Ferrari
pininfarina

First published in the United States of America in 1997
by UNIVERSE PUBLISHING
A Division of Rizzoli International Publications, Inc.
300 Park Avenue South
New York, NY 10010
and
THE VENDOME PRESS

Front cover photograph: Dino Berlinetta speciale, 1965.
© Archives Pininfarina.
Back cover photograph: Renzo Carli, Battista Pininfarina and
Sergio Pinifarina. © Archives Pininfarina.

Text and captions translated by Cynthia Calder

ISBN 0-7893-0088-5

Printed and bound in Italy

Library of Congress Catalog Card Number: 97-060141

UNIVERSE OF DESIGN

Ferrari

pininfarina

BY LIONEL FROISSART

UNIVERSE / VENDOME

Destiny is inescapable. By 1951, Enzo Ferrari had already produced some of the most impressive sports cars of the day. At the same time in Italy, Battista Pininfarina (a presidential decree authorized the name "Pininfarina" which combined Pinin, a diminutive of Battista's middle name, with Farina) was setting the standard in the field of automobile design. They realized that the time had come for them to pool their efforts. Since their first meeting thirty years earlier during a hillclimb from Aosta to the St. Bernard Pass, the two masters had crossed paths and occasionally exchanged ideas. But they had never discussed the possibility of collaborating, a concept that would later appear so self-evident. Then, in the early 1950s, Enzo Ferrari, the wizard from Maranello, decided to diversify. He wanted to find a premier "couturier" to adorn his cars, creations he likened to the loveliest Italian women. It is not surprising that both Ferrari and Pininfarina were able to recognize the obvious. These two automotive geniuses were to reap immeasurable benefits from their partnership.

When a messenger from the "house of the prancing horse" made it known that Enzo Ferrari, *Il Commendatore*, would not object to a meeting with the head of the *Carrozzeria Pininfarina*, Battista enthusiastically responded that he would be delighted to receive the great Enzo at his workshop in Turin. He proudly offered to give him a tour of the factory. But another missive informed Battista that Enzo Ferrari almost never traveled outside of Maranello. There had been a misunderstanding. The two men thought they were treating each other with the utmost tact, when in fact, neither knew the first thing about diplomacy.

It was Sergio Farina, Battista's son, who found an ideal compromise. He suggested a luncheon at a location midway between Maranello and Turin. On a map of Italy, that spot is the tiny village of Tortona. Once Pininfarina and Ferrari sat down together, the time lost in preliminary negotiations was quickly forgotten. Their desire to collaborate was sincere. Ferrari wanted to create a car with Pininfarina and the latter accepted without hesitation. The chassis and the mechanics would be Ferrari's responsibility. Pininfarina was to design the most graceful body possible without sacrificing an iota of efficiency. Sergio, who was at the luncheon, cherished wonderful memories of this day. "There was a deep mutual respect between Enzo Ferrari and my father. They knew their partnership would be profound and enduring."

After lunch, Battista got back into his Lancia Aurelia B20. Thinking over the agreement he had just reached with Ferrari, he knew that he had struck gold. Ferrari expected Pininfarina to dedicate himself wholeheartedly to this project and Battista Farina now understood that he and Ferrari would complement each other superbly. The auto industry back in Turin was less rhapsodic and more skeptical. No one expected the Pinin-Ferrari relationship to last.

Far removed from these speculations, the two men set to work. Battista Farina did not hesitate to assign this project—probably the most important of his life—to his son Sergio, an engineer fresh out of Turin's polytechnic institute. What a fabulous opportunity for a young man starting out in the family business! Sergio promptly took an office in the *l'Esperienza* design studio, where he worked ceaselessly under the rigorous expectations of his father. Meanwhile, the prestige of the Pininfarina name grew.

The marriage with Ferrari had a profound influence on the Pininfarina house. Although both firms were relatively young, each worker they employed was determined to produce cars second to none. This fundamental principle was their guide in developing a heritage of excellence. Each craftsman felt that with every stroke of the pencil or tap of the hammer, he was part of the dream that would produce the next Ferrari.

While the Ferrari racing car stable known as the *Scuderia Ferrari* was established in 1929, the Pininfarina name had slowly built its reputation from the beginning of the twentieth century, prior to the founding of the *Carrozzeria Pininfarina* in 1930. Battista Farina was born in the suburbs of Turin, in the heart of the very productive and rich Piedmont region. At the beginning of the century, the economy of this great Italian city was already largely devoted to the automobile industry. By the age of twelve, Battista was introduced into this world by his older brothers, Giovanni and Carlo, who opened a small workshop in the center of Turin. Despite competition from many other artisans, local industrialists soon noticed the fine quality of their work. Even Giovanni Agnelli, the founder of Fiat, another Turin company, had congratulated Battista Farina in person for his design of the Fiat Zero radiator and later for the body of this beautifully long, sleek touring car. With a few penstrokes, he had executed the first of many wonderful designs.

At the end of World War I, the Farina brothers' workshop again shifted into high gear. Battista Farina realized that his destiny was intertwined with the development of the automobile. Although a racing car enthusiast, Battista had more serious plans in mind. He perceived that a custom-built car had no future. It was all too rare that wealthy people came along with the means to acquire a unique and priceless car. Industrial production, he decided, was the way of the future.

So Battista decided to leave his brothers' workshop to create his own car; the *Carrozzeria Pinin Farina* was established in 1930 with its offices at 107 Corso Trapani in Turin. In addition to Fiat, he worked with almost every Italian carmaker. Battista Farina spent every day and most nights moving between his design studio and the *Carrozzeria* workshop, inspecting the curve of a hood, the final adjustments to a body panel or the last detail of a sketch. At this pace, the years passed quickly. Another world war slowed the growth of heavy industry in northern Italy. But on Christmas day in 1946 a graver crisis struck small business in Turin—fire destroyed the Corso Trapani workshop. When dawn broke, almost nothing remained of the once proud and ambitious *Carrozzeria Farina*. Only the first models of the little Cistalia had been saved, because they had been sheltered in a workshop out of the inferno's path. The Cistalia would go a long way in building the reputation of its Italian carmaker, a designer who would soon be ranked in a class of his own.

In 1951, the Cistalia 202, a bold little coupe created on Pininfarina's drawing boards, was acquired by the Museum of Modern Art in New York. The car was displayed there in its permanent collection as an automotive sculpture in motion! This success won the Italian designer the same recognition from the artistic world that he had long enjoyed from auto enthusiasts. Looking beyond all the praise and adulation, Battista Farina believed that it was the Cistalia, with its aerodynamic curves, that paved the way for much faster sports cars for him. In his autobiography *Born with the Automobile* he is quoted as saying: "For me, speed represents a never-ending exaltation."

With this background, the world waited impatiently to see the fruits of the encounter between Enzo Ferrari and Pininfarina. The *Carrozzeria* design studios had carte blanche to develop the Ferrari's sporting theme. Battista Farina, known for his extremely rigid standards, was able to eliminate "any trace of the melodramatic, the monumental or the fanciful, and above all to remove any pretentious decorative touches" from the car. Enzo Ferrari thoroughly agreed with him on these design points, which would inspire great refinements in styling.

At the beginning of the summer of 1952, barely one year after the legendary meeting in Tortona, the first Ferrari bodied by Pininfarina was unveiled—the 212 Inter. This cabriolet initially experienced a few minor problems with its proportions because of the unusual size of the Ferrari engine, but these details were quickly ironed out. At its debut, the car exhibited a striking sleekness. The first 212 Inter chassis was sent to Switzerland for a client identified as George Filipinetti, one of the earliest Ferrari enthusiasts. This model (of which only seventeen were produced) combined excellence in automotive styling with a mastery of the technical complexities of a sports cars.

The early Ferrari-Pininfarina partnership was extremely prosperous. Their cars received a spectacular welcome at the auto shows. Following the introduction of the 212 Inter at the Brussels show, Pininfarina presented the 375 MM in Turin. In the designer's own words, these cars were the first two "children" from the marriage of passion and reason between Ferrari and the "artists' workshop" of Turin.

At the 1954 Paris Auto Show two new models created by the car designer graced the Ferrari stand—the 250 GT Berlinetta and the 375 America Berlinetta. The 250 GT Berlinetta is without doubt one of the most beautiful cars ever designed. The 375 America Berlinetta gleamed under the roof of the Grand Palais; behind the wheel was one of the most dedicated admirers of the prancing horse emblem—Ingrid Bergman.

By this juncture, Enzo Ferrari and Pininfarina had moved beyond the stage of simple technical and commercial collaboration. Although they did not like to discuss it, they were united by a yearning to work together. Pininfarina tirelessly churned out designs until he created his own distinct style. This style has grown so successful that today a Ferrari is instantly recognizable. It can be distinguished easily from other touring sports cars. And it need not always be red (the Italian racing team's color of the day) or yellow (the color of Modena) to confirm its identity. This impassioned partnership has indeed made a greater contribution to the development of the sports car than was ever expected at the outset.

As he continued to prosper, Pininfarina realized he had to modernize his plant to handle the constant and heavy flow of orders. But he recognized that he could not lose any creativity, his most important raw material. The activities of Pininfarina, his son Sergio and his son-in-law Renzo expanded as they acquired the capacity to operate on a scale competitive with the biggest companies. With extraordinary vision, they planned an enormous wind tunnel in the middle of the new factory to be built in the outskirts of Turin, with a view over the Alps. They knew that the power and majesty of the mountains would surely inspire their designers' imagination.

As the 1960s approached, Battista Farina had paved the way to a smooth future. His personality had contributed enduring support to the foundations of the great firm which had prospered under his leadership. His son Sergio summarized the situation very well, commenting on the place his father held in the automotive world: "He created everything for the Pininfarina name. He was like a vast lake, flowing over everyone and everything. It was impossible to swim to the shore."

But, starting in 1965, it was Sergio Pininfarina and Renzo Carli who, in addition to handling the general management of the company, turned their creative energy to the next Ferrari, a car that would soon be known as the "little" Ferrari 246 GT. This was a project that Pininfarina and Ferrari would never have attempted. Reviewing the latest sketches of the Dino, Pininfarina remarked: "This Dino is exactly the kind of bold design I hoped my sons would create. The newest plans or systems are always the best, the ones created by young people. Here is a car that will challenge anyone who believes that good taste is on its last legs in our business." However, the Dino made history in another way. This very compact car, with its sensuous curves, was powered by an engine newly designed by Alfredino, Enzo Ferrari's beloved son, who was dying. It was from his hospital bed that "Dino" conceived and designed this small 6-cylinder car, powered by three twin-choke Weber carburetors.

But the most revolutionary aspect of the Dino was not visible on the surface. For the first time since the beginning of their fruitful collaboration, the Ferrari technicians, the chief Ferrari engineer and the Pininfarina designers disagreed over a technical issue. They were unable to compromise for weeks on end. While Pininfarina wanted to build a car with a mid-mounted engine, Enzo Ferrari considered the idea preposterous. Ferrari believed that the engines in his racing cars had to be placed in front of the driver, insisting that no other position was acceptable. This presented a thorny problem. Enzo Ferrari's personality was as strong as his ideas. No one knows how Pininfarina was able to convince the builder from Maranello to depart from his principles for once. But he did finally agree to allow a midengined layout on the Dino, a revolutionary concept for this Ferrari that was not configured for racing. Enzo Ferrari offered no further input into the design of this machine.

Dino Ferrari died from a virus at an early age and never heard the roar of the distinctive engine he designed. After the sad passing of his son, Ferrari's character became tougher than ever. Legend has it that Enzo completed his son's work at his gravesite in Modena's cemetery.

The prototype for the Dino Berlinetta Special was presented at the Paris Auto Show in 1965. The Dino GT and the 206 GT were subsequently launched with great triumph. Their innovation received unanimous praise, and loyal clients of the "prancing horse" were not disappointed. With the passing of time, Sergio Pininfarina came to think of the Dino as a seminal creation of the Ferrari-Pininfarina partnership; this Berlinetta strongly influenced the design of future sports cars, no matter who made them. With its center-mounted engine the Ferrari broke new ground and revolutionized the sports car. The Dino, which remained in the catalogue for twenty years (an exceptionally long life, even for such an exclusive car), also carried with it a uniquely personal, touching story.

Battista Pininfarina also departed the stage before the Dino's story was complete. He died in a Lausanne clinic while the

Ferrari designed by his sons was taking shape on the drawing boards. On April 3, 1966, Battista Pininfarina left the world as he had predicted, at peace with himself. His body lay in state in the Pininfarina factory. Enzo Ferrari made the trip to Turin that he had never before attempted. He had to pay his last respects to his friend, the master. The association of their two names had contributed so much to the world of the automobile.

"Now, we must speak to each other in the informal fashion," he said simply to Sergio Pininfarina upon leaving the room where his father's body lay. Enzo Ferrari offered this privilege only rarely. It was his way of letting the Pininfarina heir know that he had earned his confidence.

Now at the helm, Sergio Pininfarina dedicated himself to maintaining the identity of his business. He wisely assigned creative responsibilities to young designers, recognizing that "I can no longer devote all my time to designing as my father once did. Nor do I want to abandon my creative role. My responsibility is to lead by inspiration." While instinct inspired the creator of Pininfarina, Sergio, with his technical training, introduced more discipline into the firm.

The story continues, with no barriers to its continuing prosperity. In 1968, Ferrari introduced the magnificent 365 GTB/4, better known under the simple name the "Daytona". This large Berlinetta with its superb front-mounted 12 cylinder engine was an unfortunate victim of its own success. It quickly became a collector's item and only very rarely does its streamlined silhouette grace the roads. Today the Daytona is best remembered for its characteristically elongated hood and elegant lines enhanced by a few fine details that contributed so greatly to its success. The perfection of this body has not faded with time; it remains yet another successful combination of beauty and aggressive design, with no hint of ostentation. The harshest critics can't help but admire such a creation, which combines an expansively long nose, in breathtaking harmony with a simple, sensually abbreviated rear section.

The Pininfarina-Ferrari line went from one triumph to another. Every debut was greeted with admiration. The ingenious designers of Turin managed ceaselessly to surprise and innovate while complying with increasingly rigorous technological and safety constraints. Even for someone who is not a Ferrari devotee, these cars from Maranello are always a sight to behold, often capable of sparking love at first sight. There is real magic—in the truest sense—in that discreet Pininfarina badge on the lower side of the body. The mystique remains and the fascination continues to grow.

Four years after the Daytona, Pininfarina demonstrated the open-mindedness of its designers. The Paris Auto Show was the showcase for a new wonder, the 365 GT4. Designed to carry four passengers, it did not compromise any of the feel of a sports car. Its proportions became even more refined with the creation of the 2+2 coupe (automatic!) followed by the 412 with its enticing elegance. Few aficionados of the prancing horse could criticize cars of such rare purity and simplicity. The 412 was one of the most mainstream Ferraris ever produced. An even more sumptuous version could have been made but Enzo Ferrari himself vetoed the idea. To commemorate the fiftieth anniversary of Pininfarina, the designer wanted to create the Pinin, an impressive four-door Berlinetta powered by a large, 12-cylinder, five-liter Ferrari engine. In Ferrari's mind, this concept strayed too far from his vision of a sports car. Displayed at the Turin Auto Show, the four-seater Pinin was merely a stylistic exercise.

This "disappointment" was no more than a brief episode for Pininfarina, who then undertook the development of what would become the Testarossa in 1984, a triumph unforeseen by even the most optimistic fans. It was obvious that the Testarossa was utterly performance-oriented. It followed the 512BB, which was much admired by dedicated Ferrari devotees. The Pininfarina workshops were geared up to turn out two of these models a day. At peak demand, seven cars a day made their first runs on the Via Abetone for the traditional test drive before delivery.

The idea behind the Testarossa was to update an older model with a bolder look. The flow of air across the radiators affected the design of the side grilles, which were dominated by two large "conveyors," accentuating the car's powerful, aggressive image. These two parameters defined this model's outstanding characteristics.

The Testarossa successfully embodied the mystique that was an intrinsic part of many cars bearing the prancing horse emblem. All Ferrari buyers found their own gratification with the purchase. Buyers included royalty, devoted fanatics, those who viewed the acquisition of a Ferrari bodied by Pininfarina as the affirmation of a certain kind of power and self-image. The introduction of the 456 GT in 1992 was an excellent example of how far Ferrari had come in expanding the versatility of its line. This 2+2 intended to reestablish the correct distance, which had diminished year by year, between the classic Ferrari Grand Touring cars and other upscale cars. The 456 once again exuded the Ferrari spirit, which cannot be fully expressed in words. It is easy to distinguish a Ferrari from other four-wheel vehicles, as it is transformed by an "entire system of symbols that belong to a rich, vibrant heritage. There is a stylistic coherence to the whole, a judicious amount of innovation combined with a respect for tradition," a Pininfarina designer once explained. With each new Ferrari, the Pininfarina artists were challenged to outdo themselves yet again.

Pininfarina also observed the important dates in Ferrari's history. The F40, of which 1300 models were built, marked the Maranello company's fortieth anniversary. This was the last model overseen by Enzo Ferrari before his death in 1988. The F40 was also one of the few Ferraris designed by Pininfarina in which certain aspects of the car's styling were sacrificed for aerodynamic considerations. Logically enough, the F50 was created ten years later. With its distinctive race car look, it was directly inspired by the Formula 1 car. The F50 was the first sports car ever built that dared deploy the know-how and materials associated with the most sophisticated racing technology.

The driving performance of this projectile powered by a V-12 engine with over 500 horsepower made the F50 the ultimate car of its genre. This caused much disappointment since the car was reserved for only 349 privileged people. But then came the Maranello 550. Introduced at the 1996 Paris Auto Show, it demonstrated how the roots of Pininfarina and Ferrari's labor were deep and strong. In this model, Ferrari combined the front-mounted motor of a Berlinetta with dynamic sports car performance. With the Testarossa as forerunner, Pininfarina conceived an extremely high performance car designed to exhilarate the driver (now the pilot) without neglecting the quality and comfort of life on board. The Italian designer wanted the Maranello 550 to be a car that was both futuristic and rational.

The Turin designers made wide use of subtleties to distinguish themselves from any possible competition. Thus the 550 Maranello—whose austere lines were praised when it was introduced—benefited from several decisive penstrokes which demonstrated the close cooperation between the two partners. All the solutions which had been analyzed and explored by Ferrari were affirmed and refined by Pininfarina.

The result is inscribed in history: an austere, efficient and functional style, universally recognizable. It is a form of simple expressiveness that conveys beauty to the automobile.

As we approach the new millennium, it seems clear that the Pininfarina adventure is nowhere near its close. Like all success stories, the episodes follow one after another, never ceasing. Better yet, the future has been secured. Sergio Pininfarina, who is looking forward to more leisure time, has already handed over the reins to his sons Andrea and Paolo, as his father had to do himself years ago. So, as Ferrari celebrates its centennial, it is a safe wager that the model marking this anniversary will bear the Pininfarina badge. Much to the eye's delight.

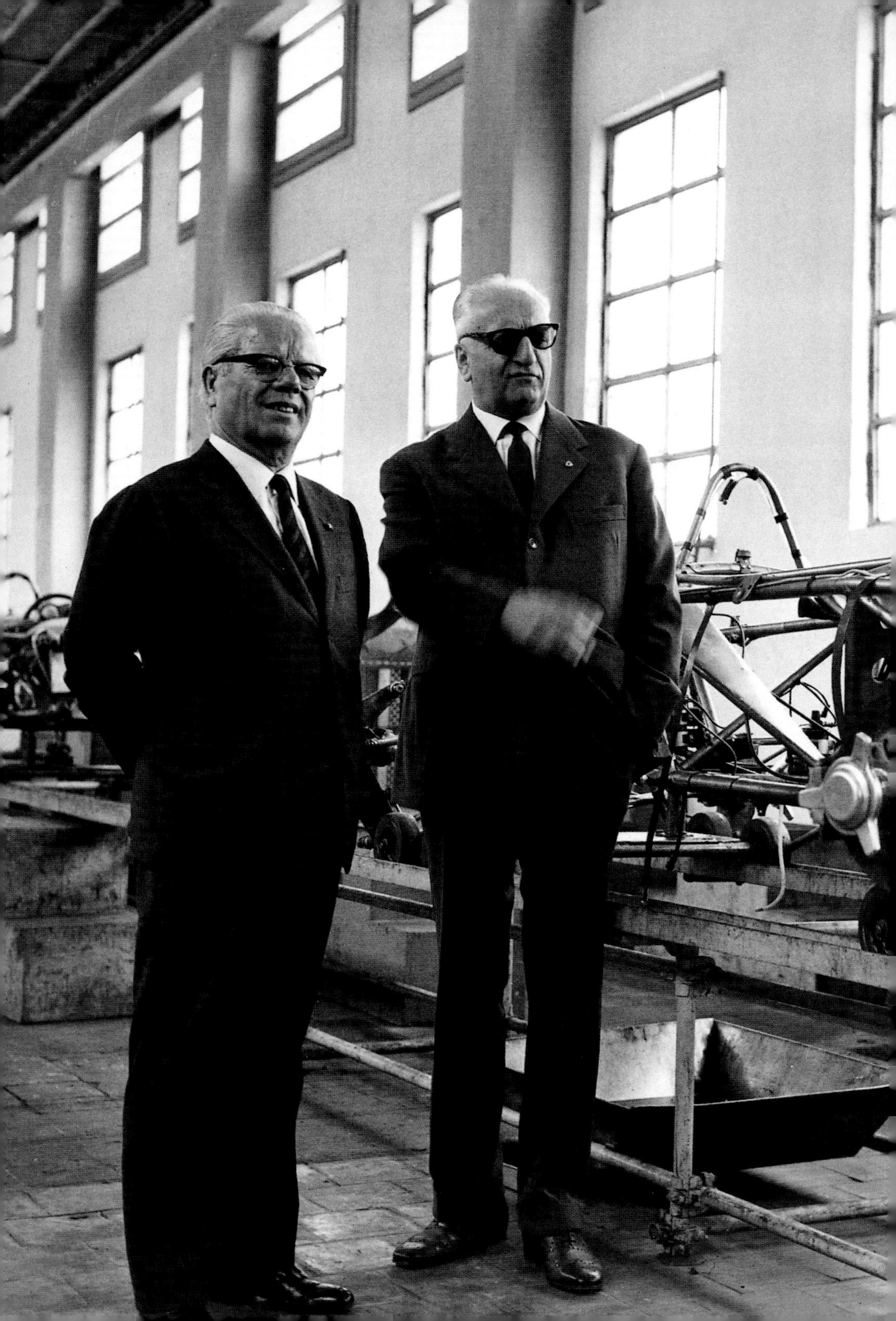

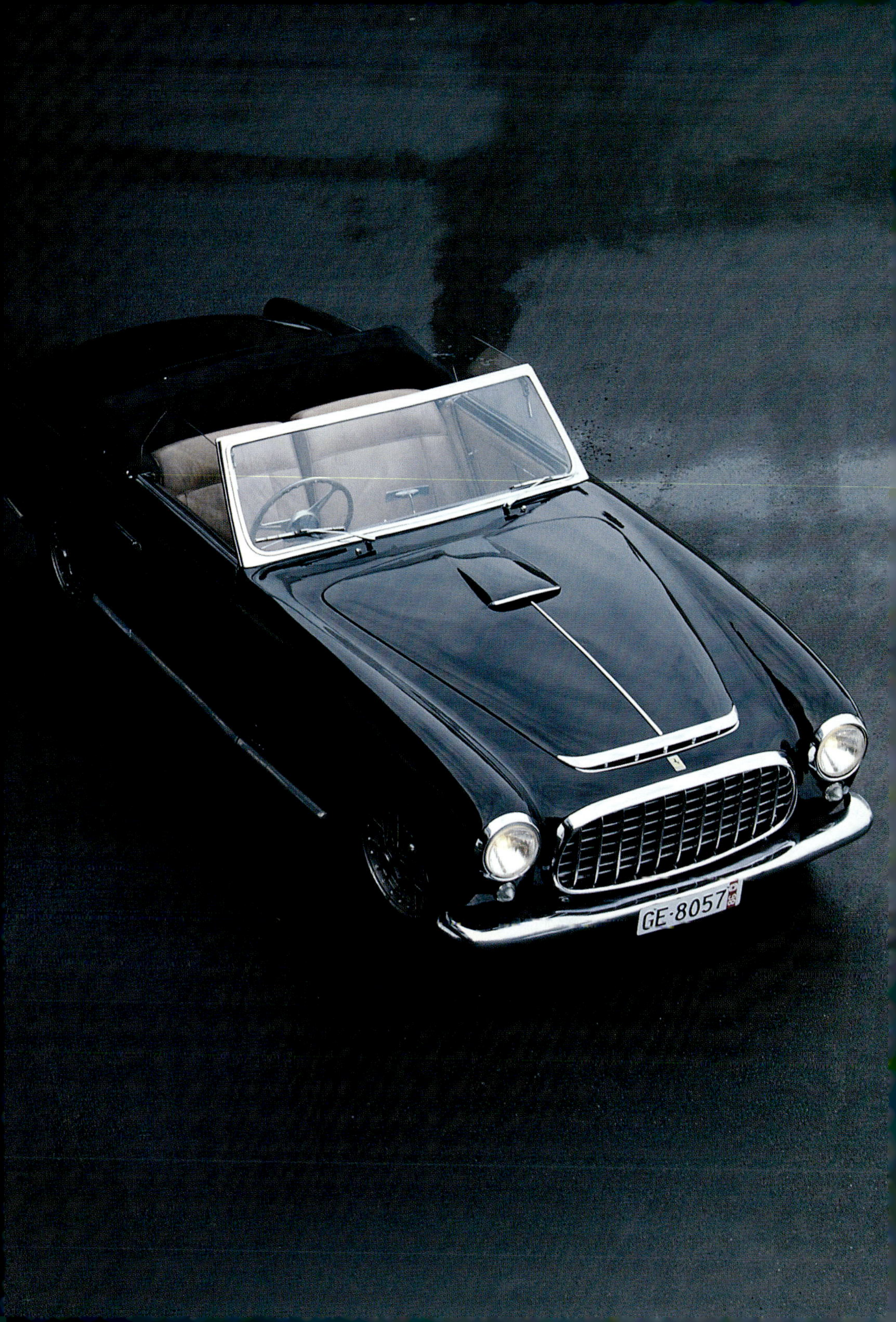
GE-8057

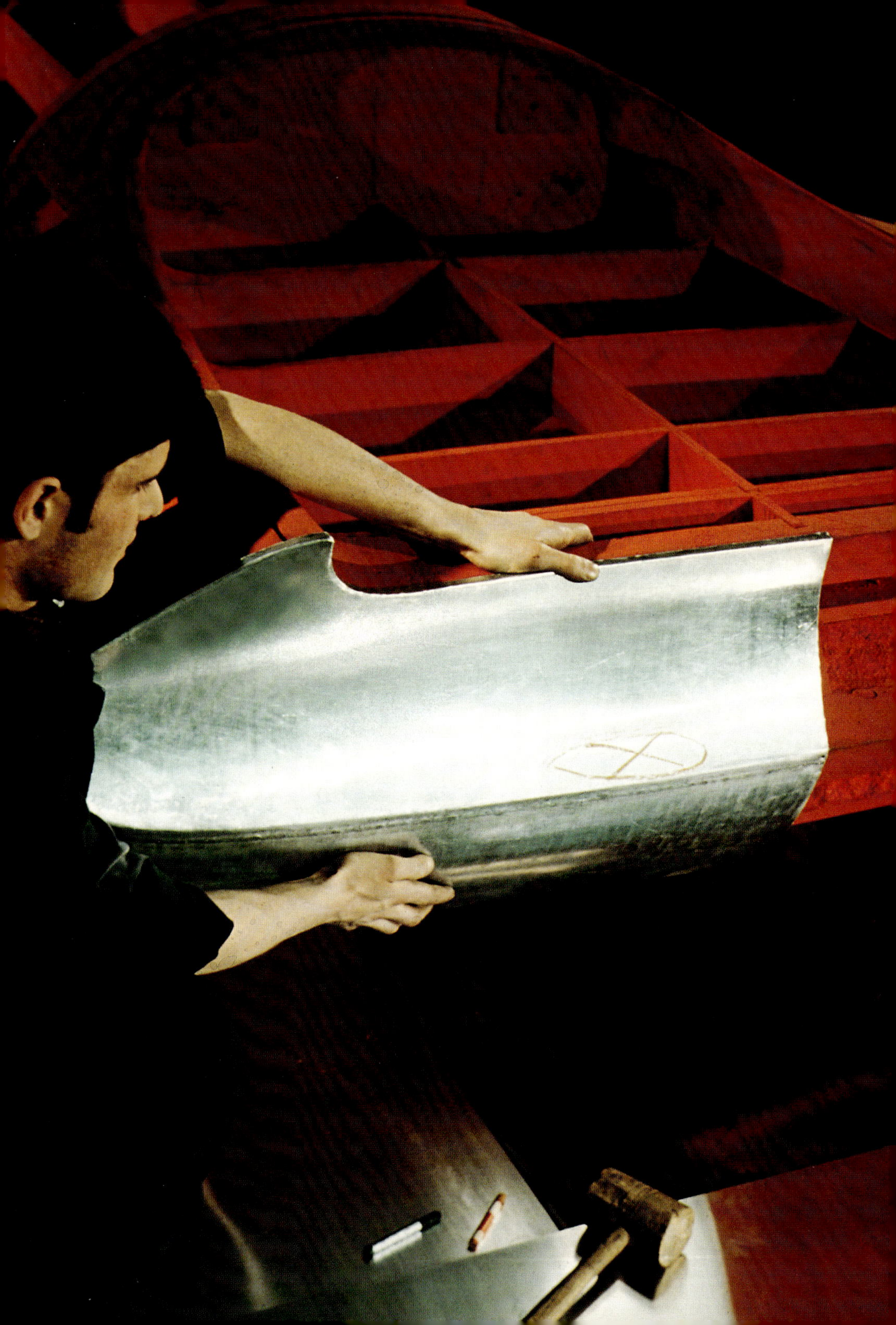

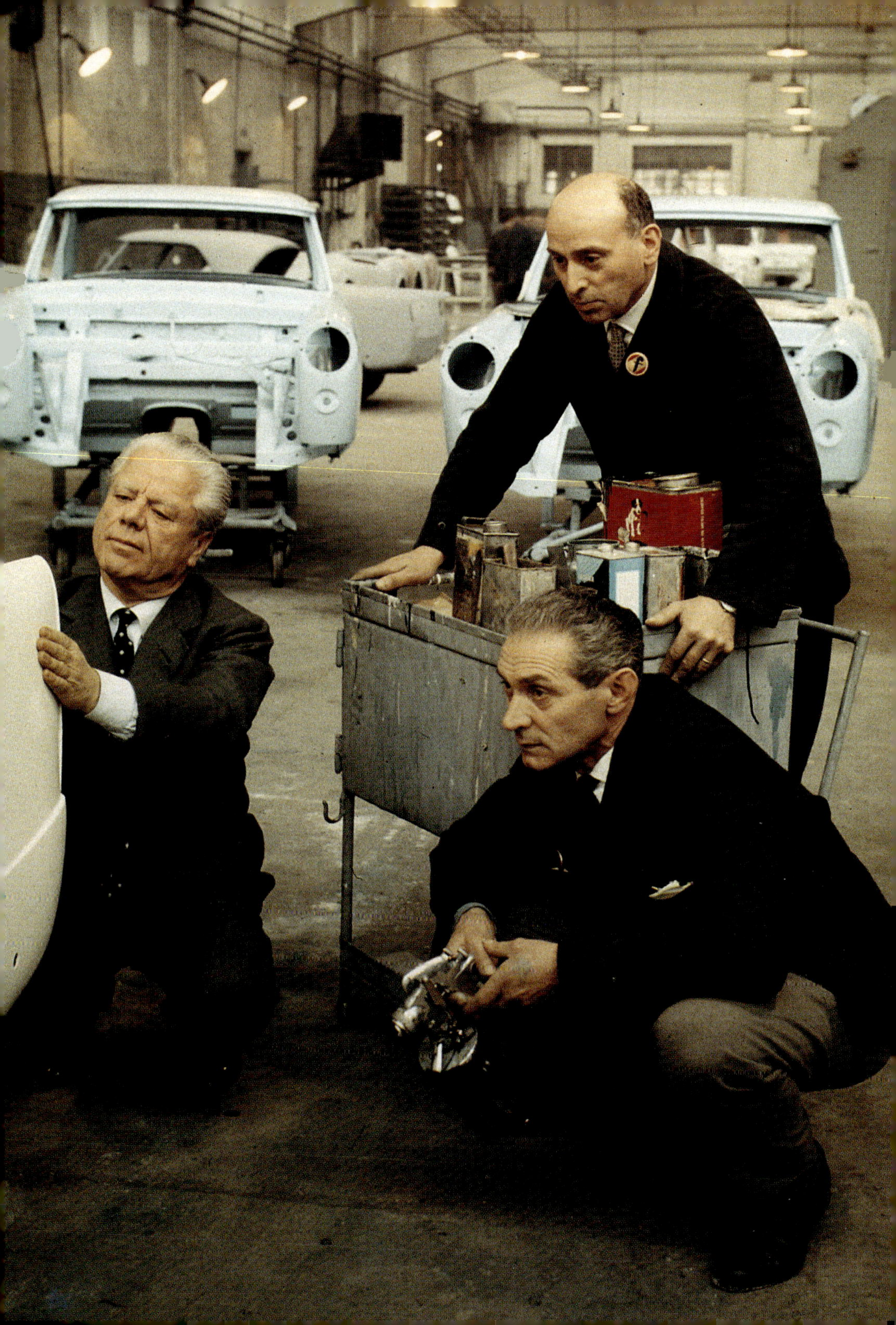

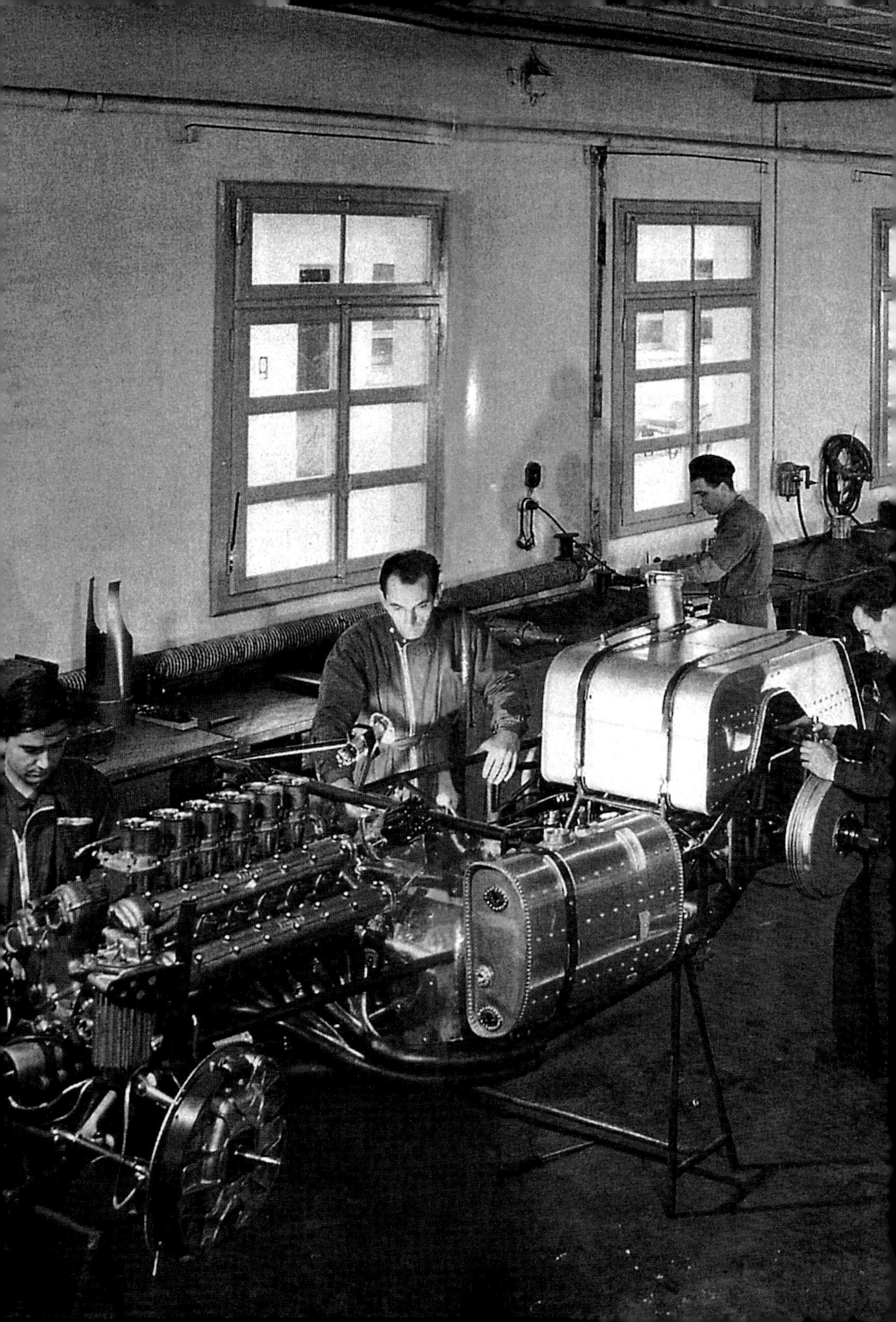

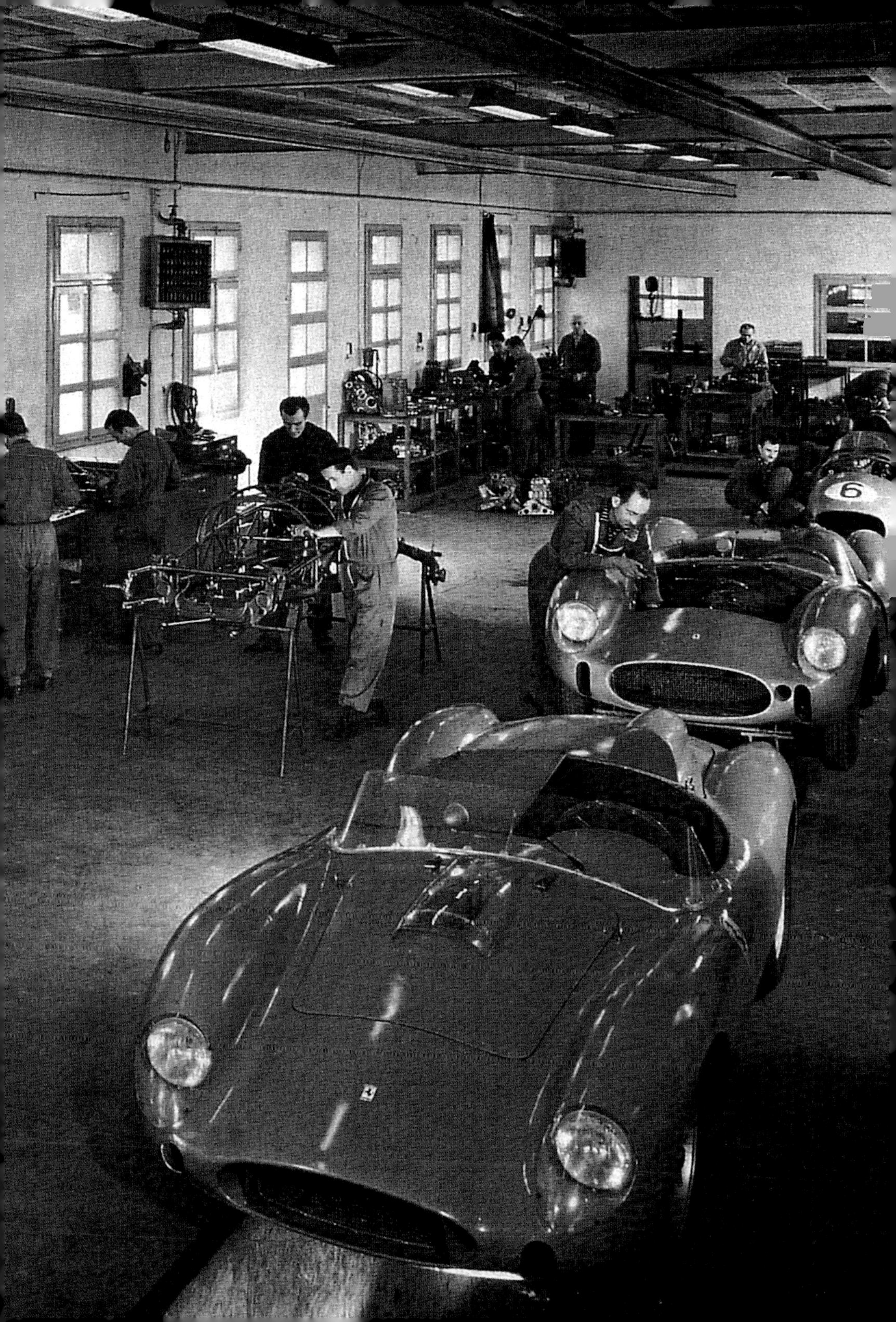
6

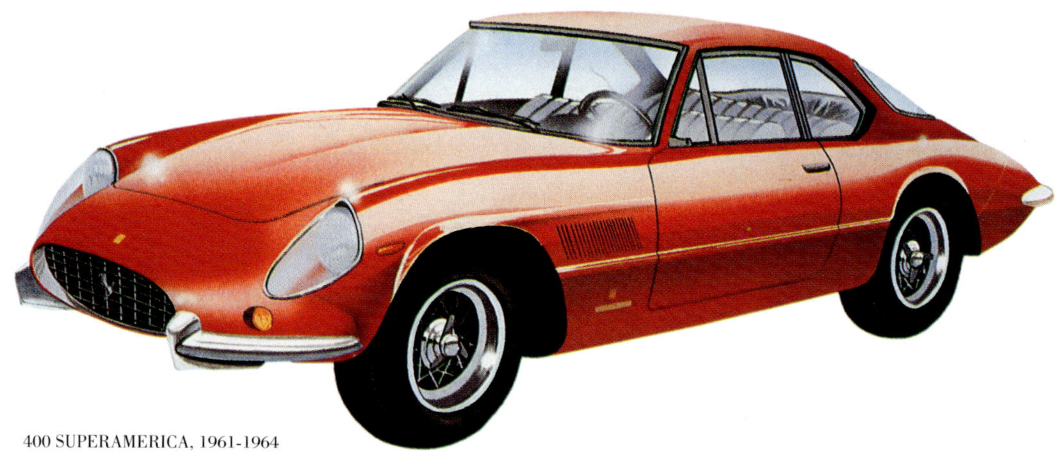

400 SUPERAMERICA, 1961-1964

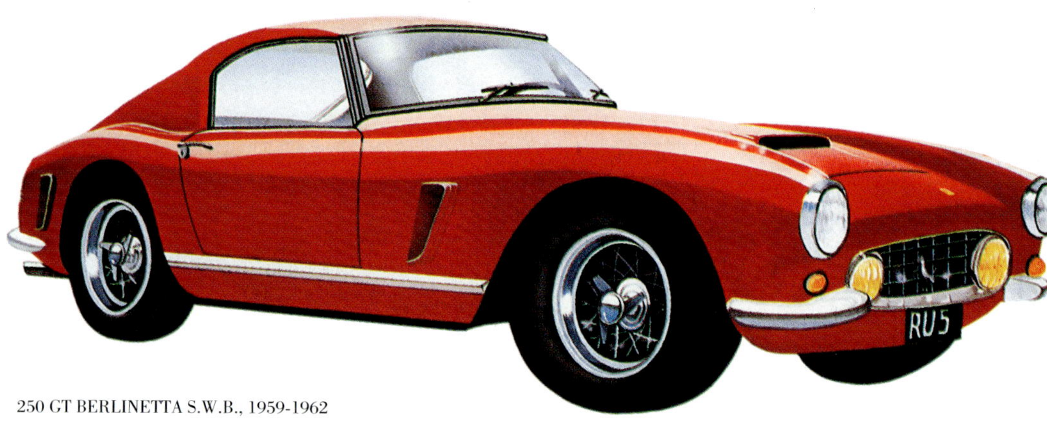

250 GT BERLINETTA S.W.B., 1959-1962

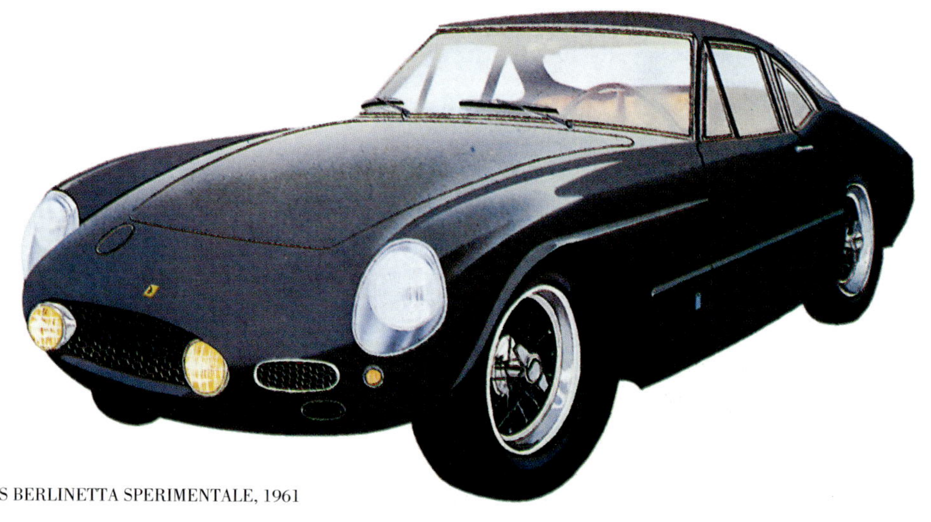

LE MANS BERLINETTA SPERIMENTALE, 1961

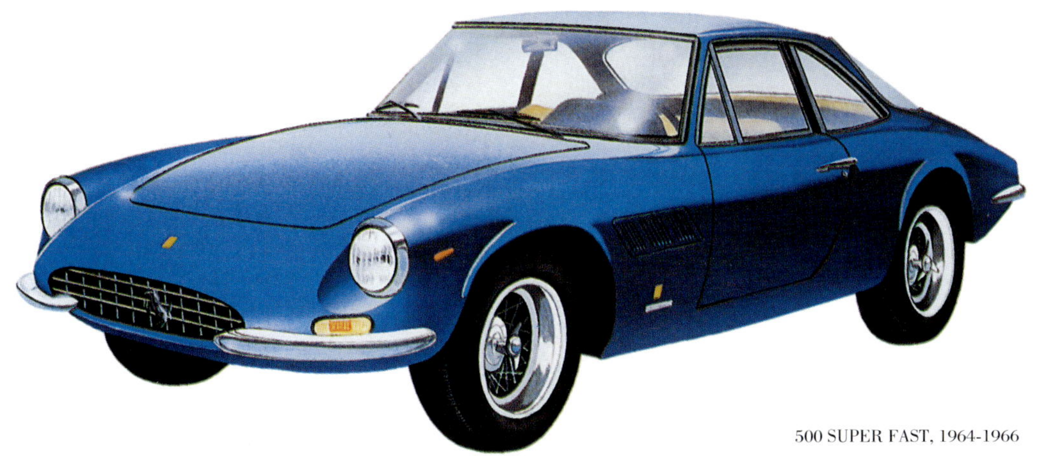

500 SUPER FAST, 1964-1966

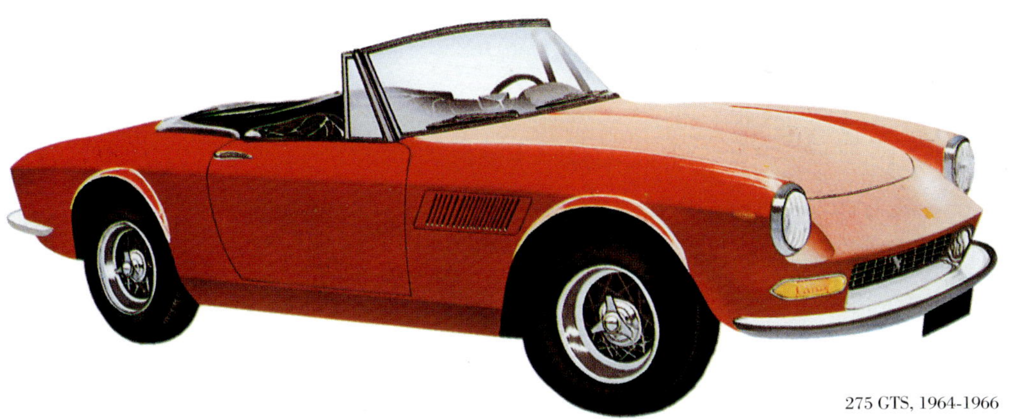

275 GTS, 1964-1966

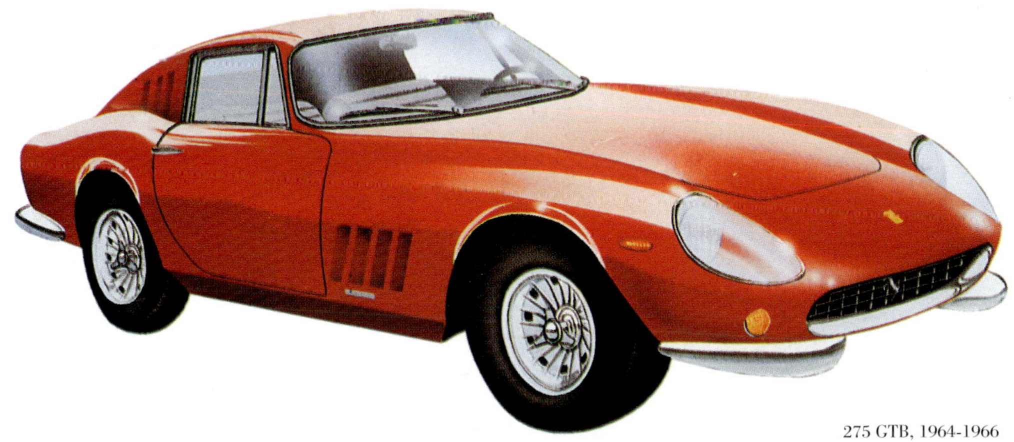

275 GTB, 1964-1966

AMPIONI
O SPORT
ARLANO

miracolo a Marane

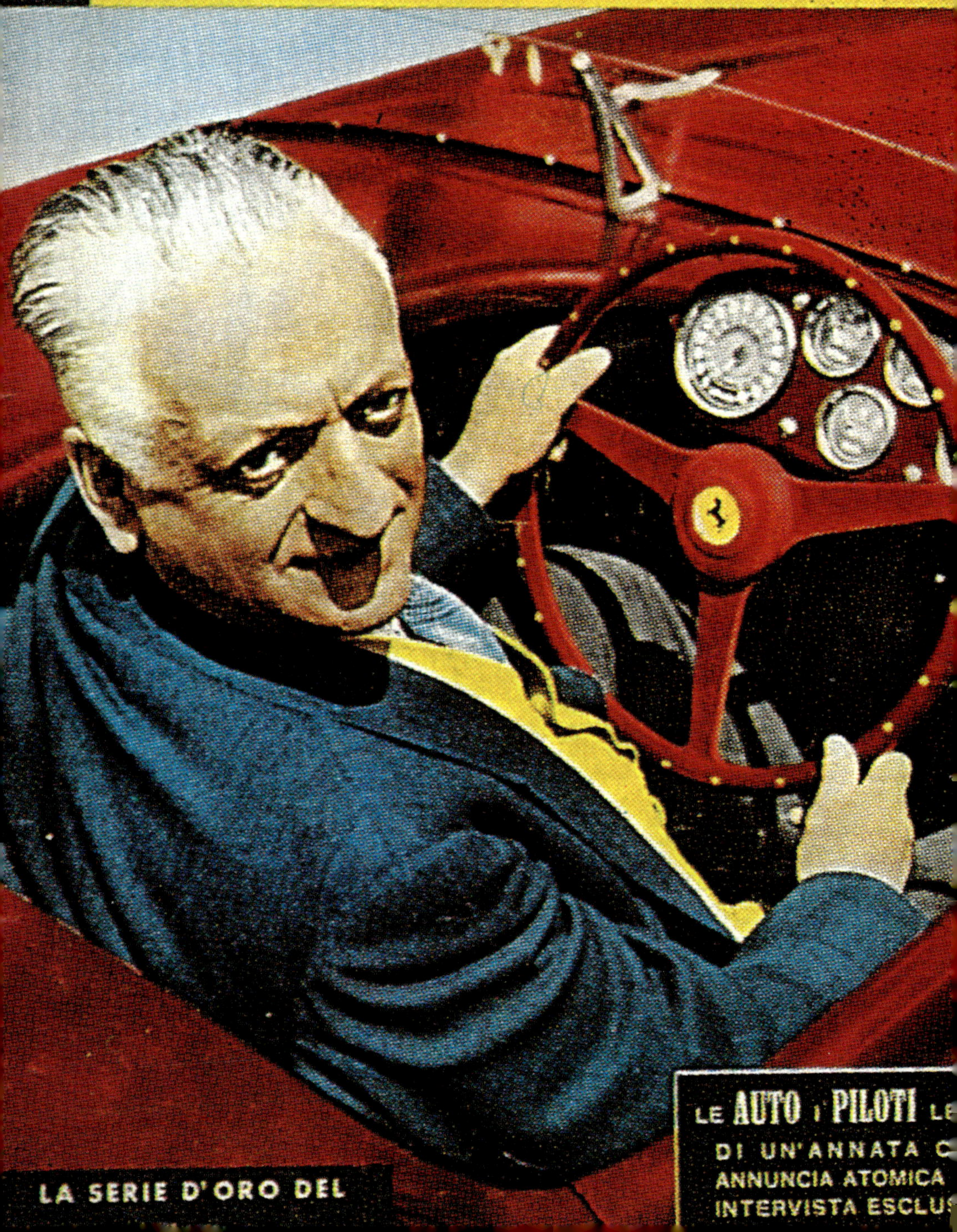

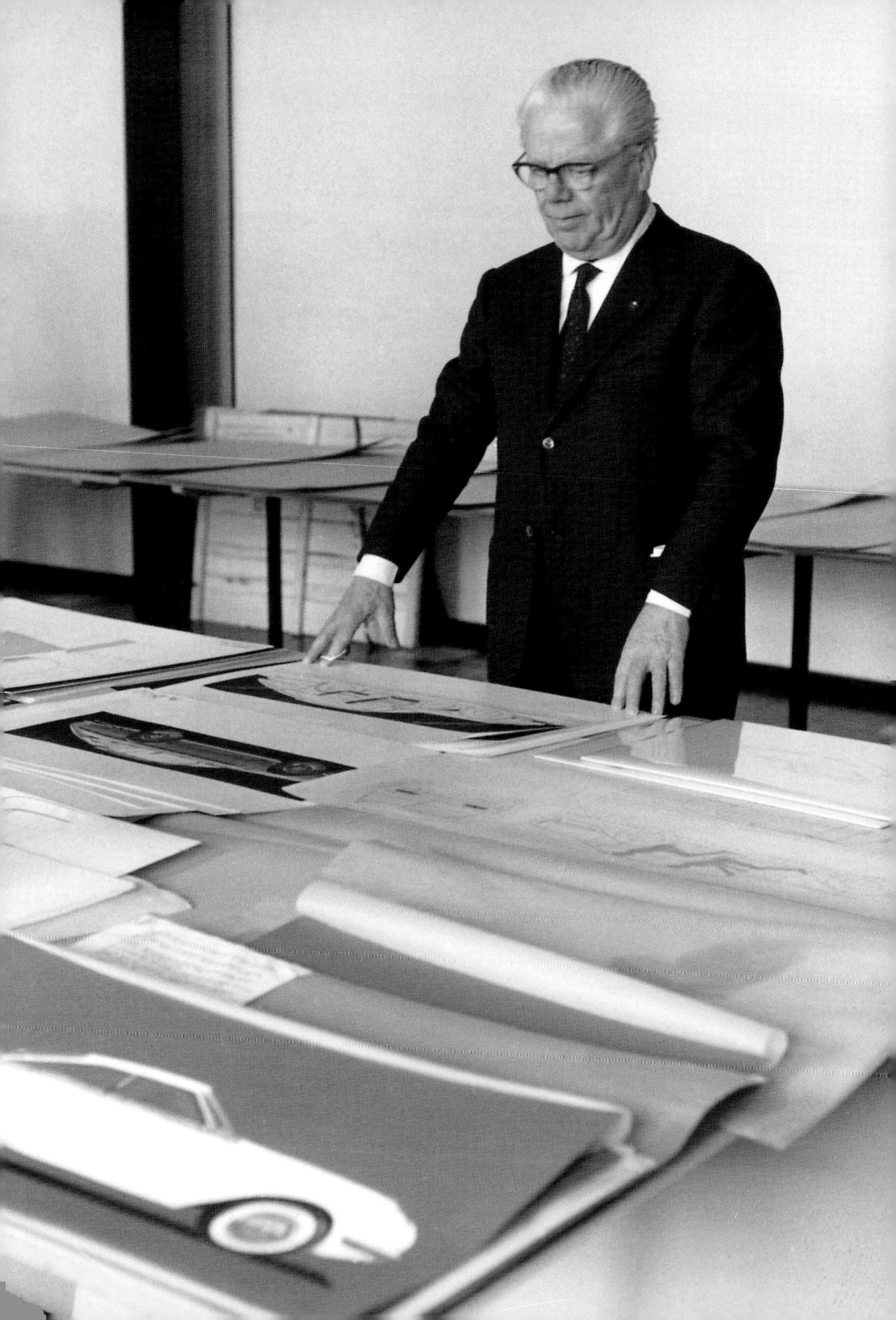

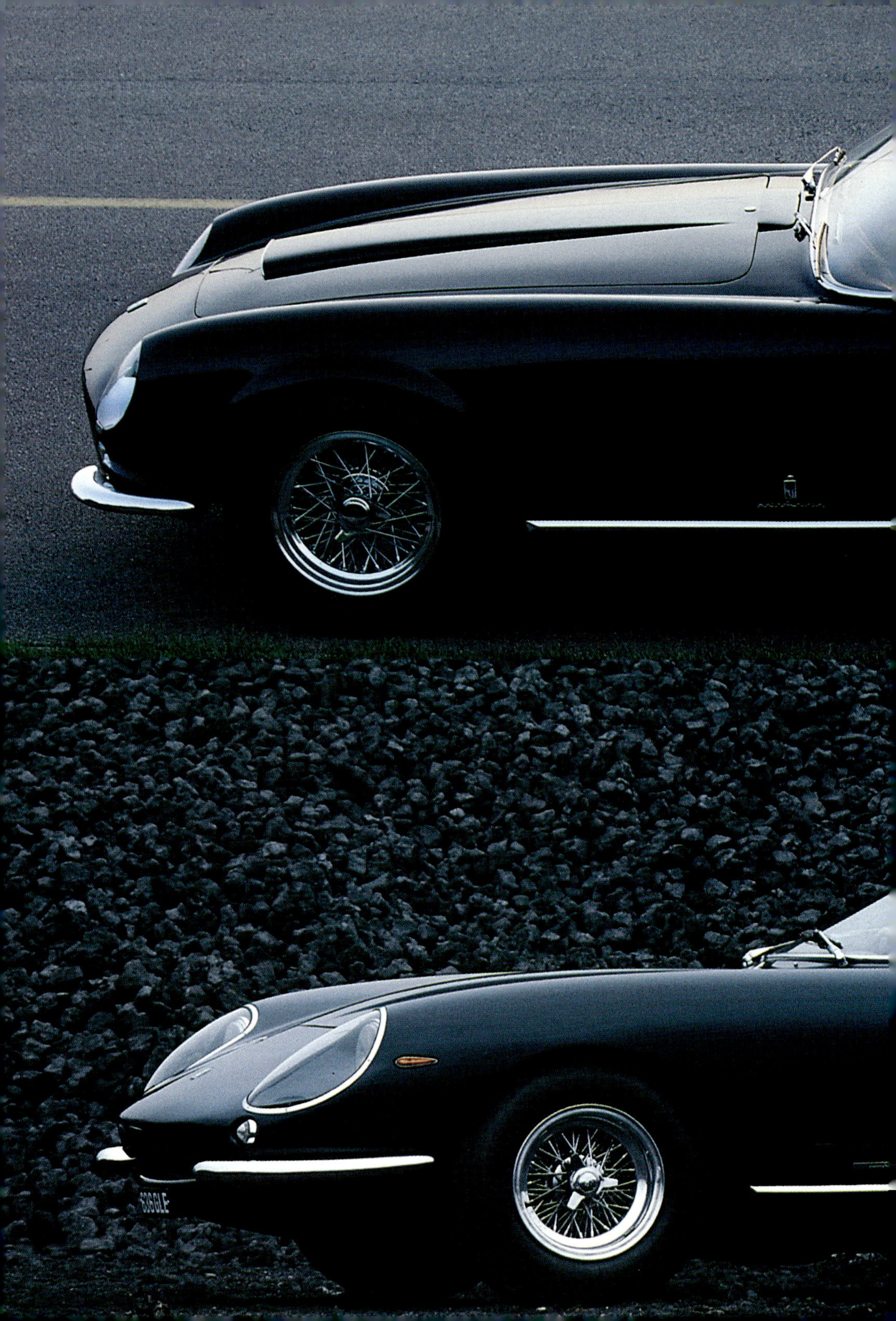

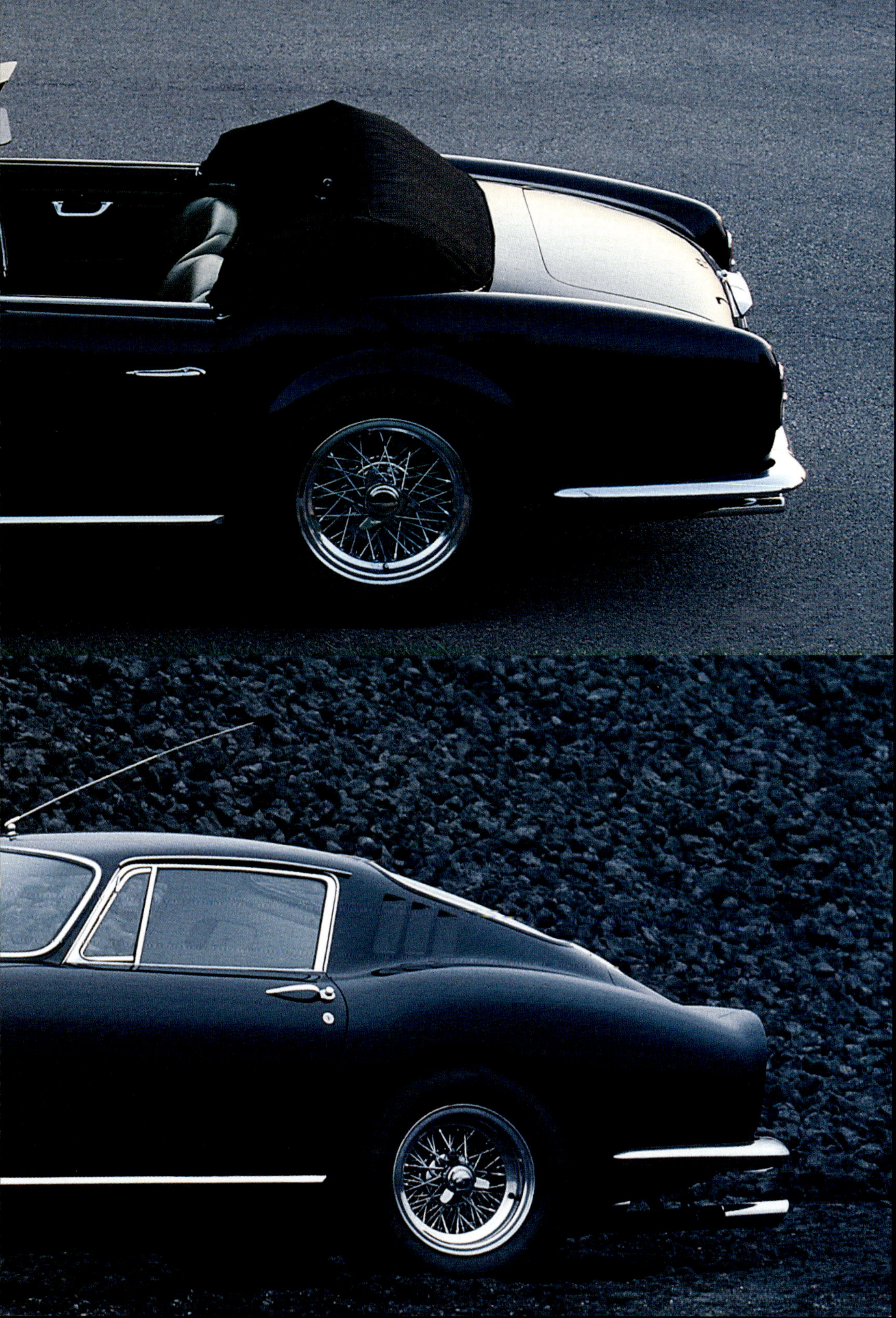

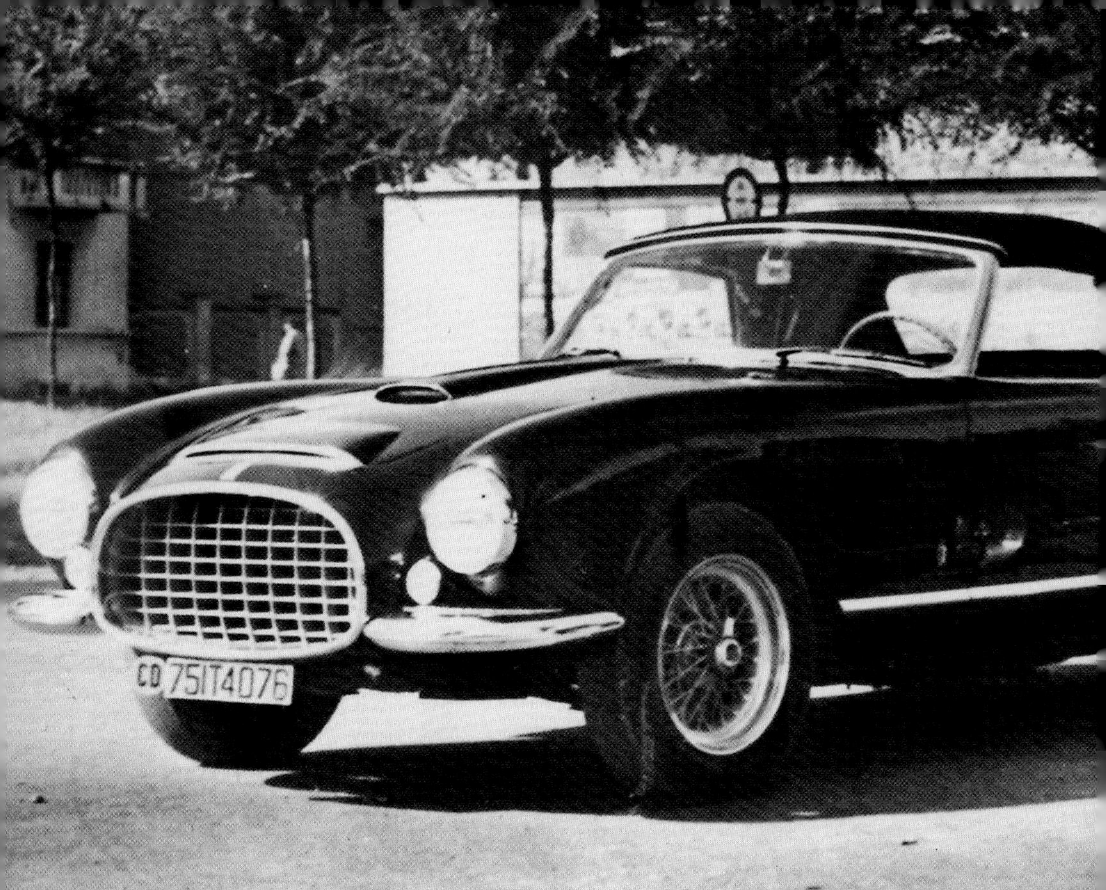

A Monsieur Pinin Farina

En souvenir de deux de

Le

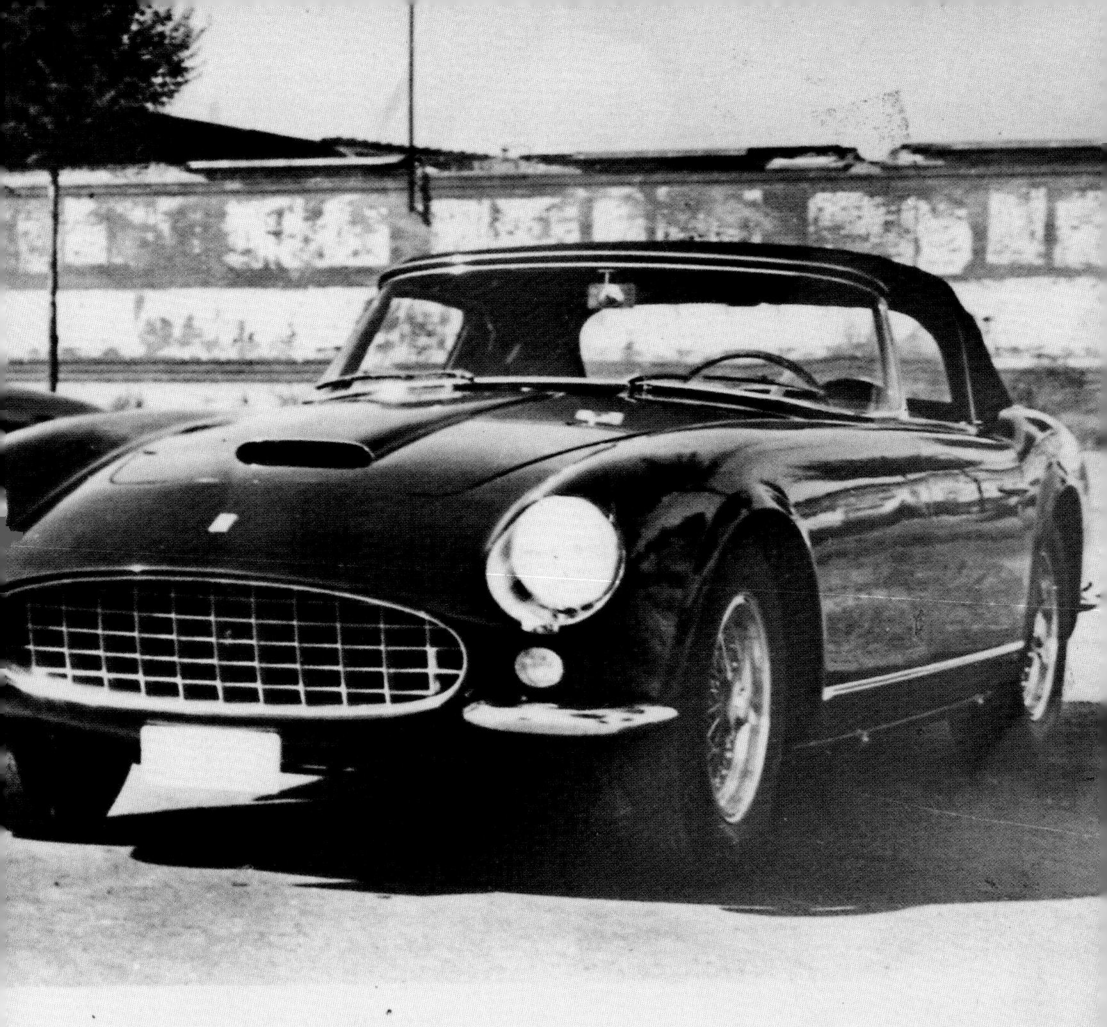

plus beaux enfants

Turin, le 8 Octobre 1955

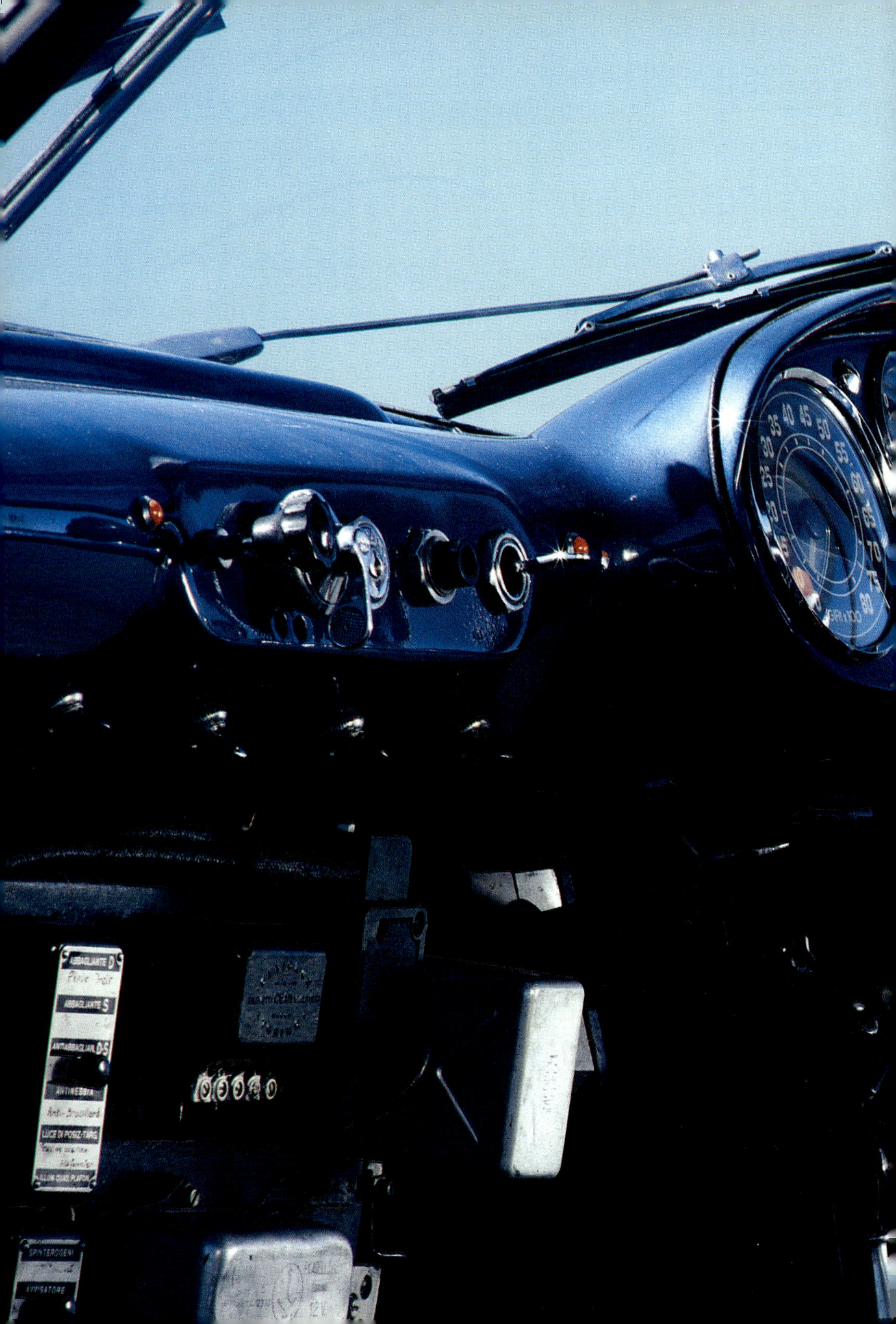

35 40 45 50 55 60 65 70 75 80
GIRI x 100
ABBAGLIANTE D
ABBAGLIANTE S
ANTIABBAGLIAN. D-S
ANTINEBBIA
Anti-Brouillard
LUCE DI POSIZ-TARG.
SPINTEROGENO
AVVISATORE

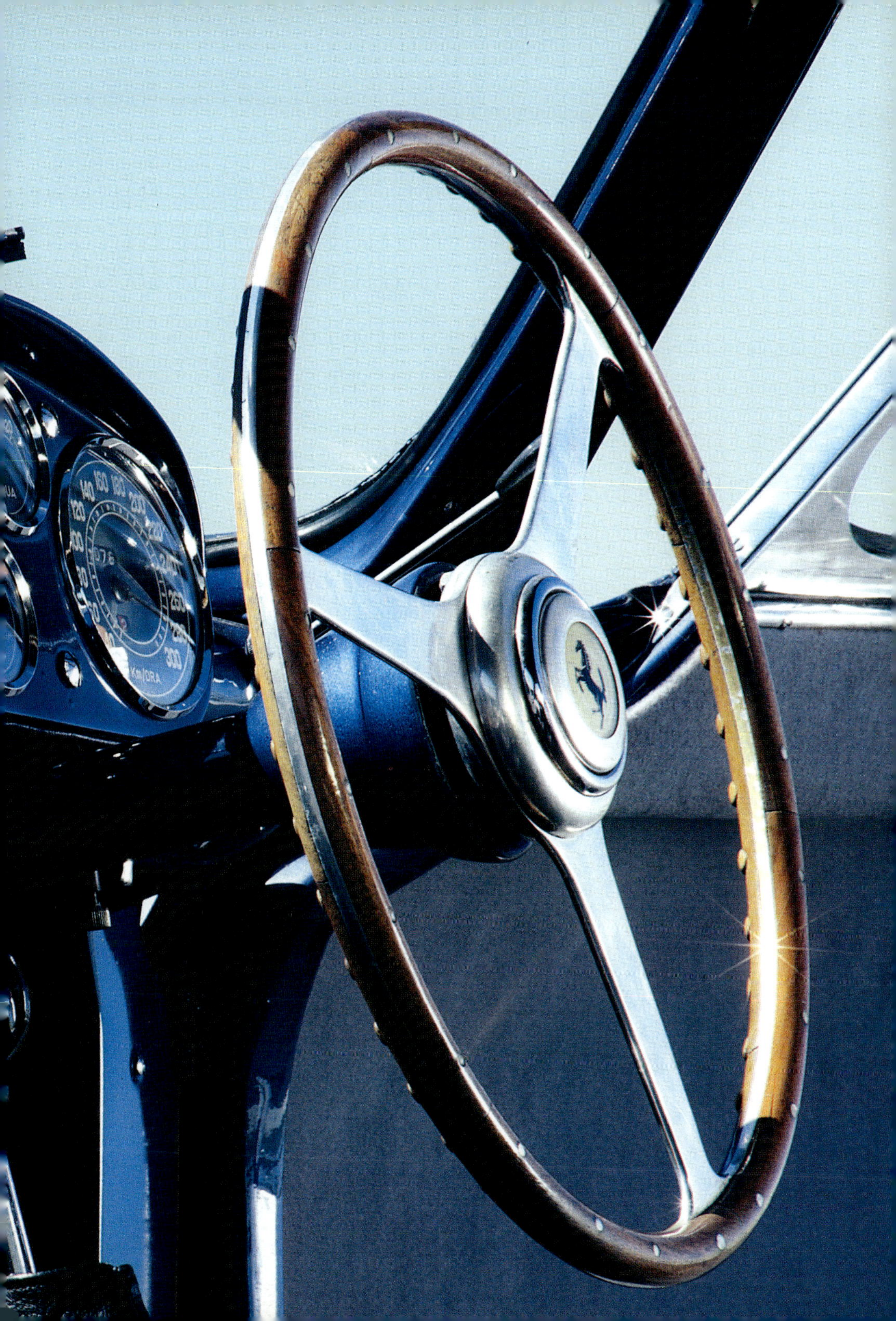
Km/ORA

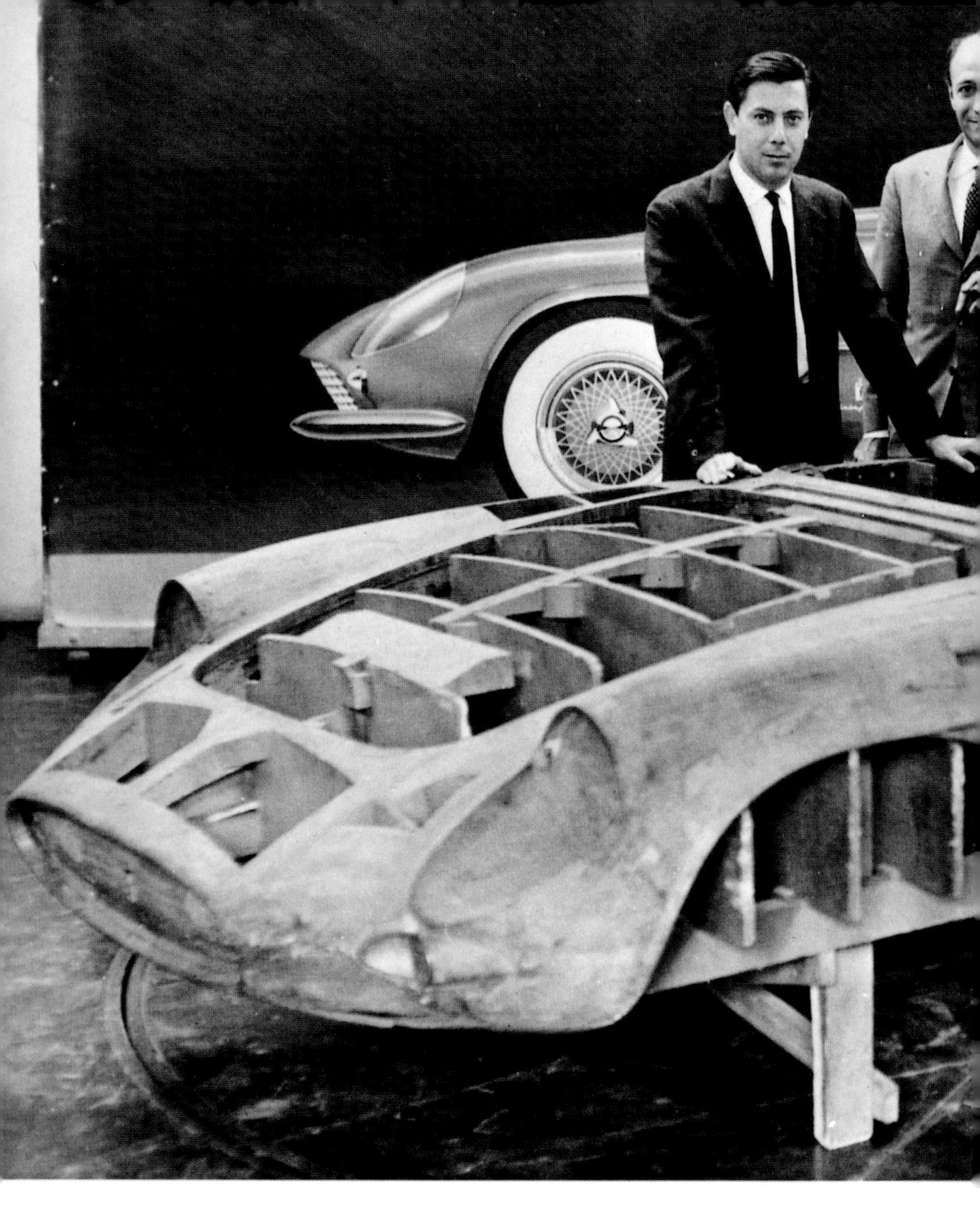

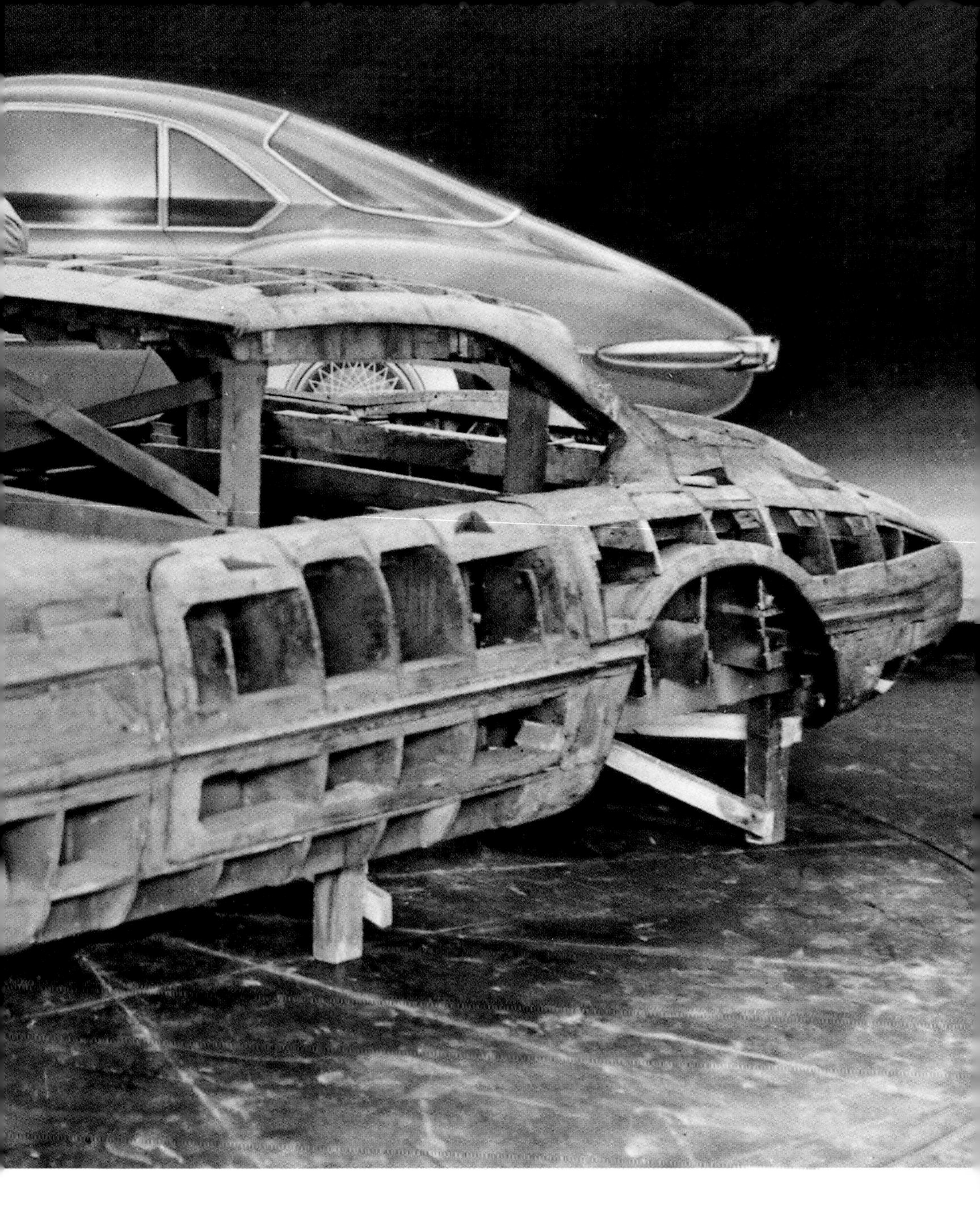

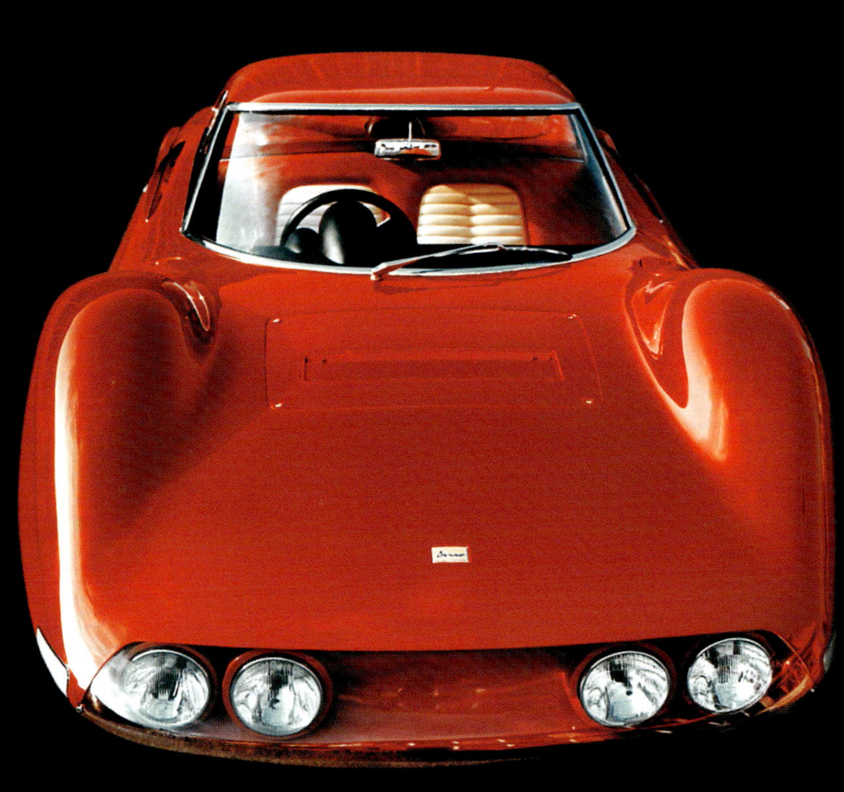

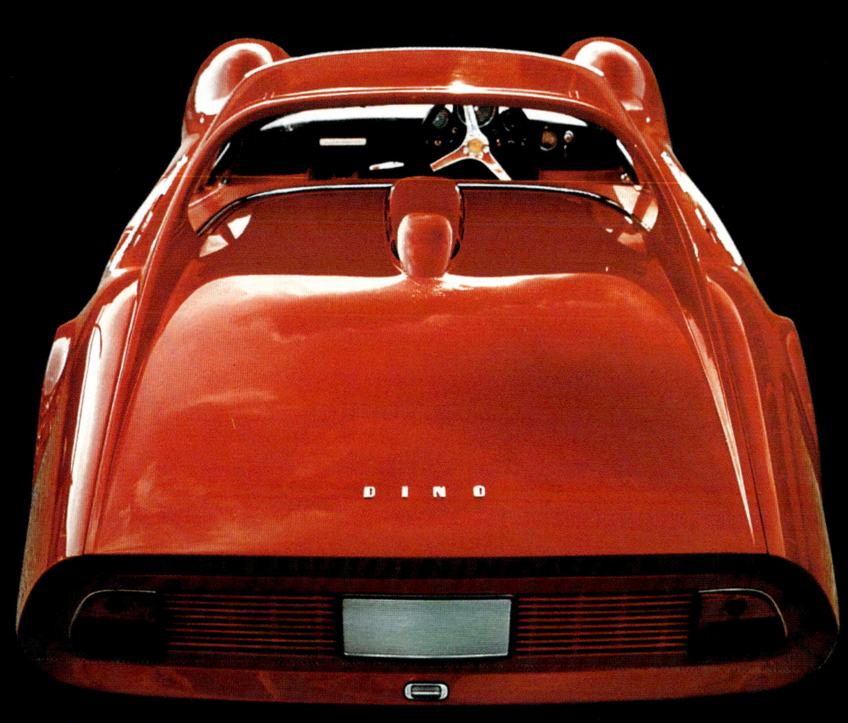
DINO

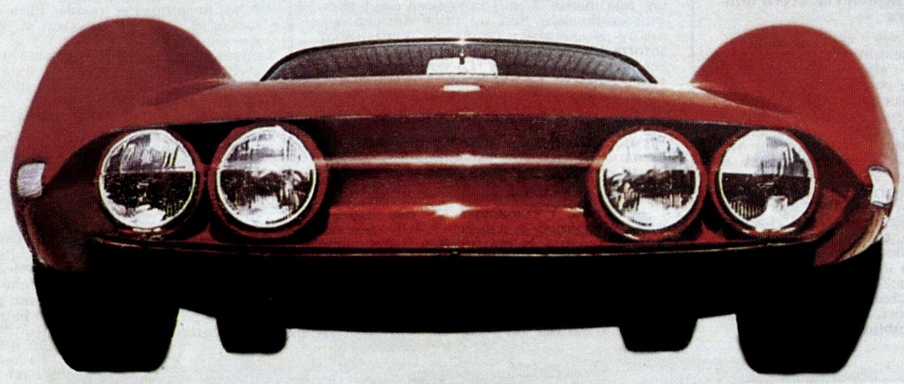

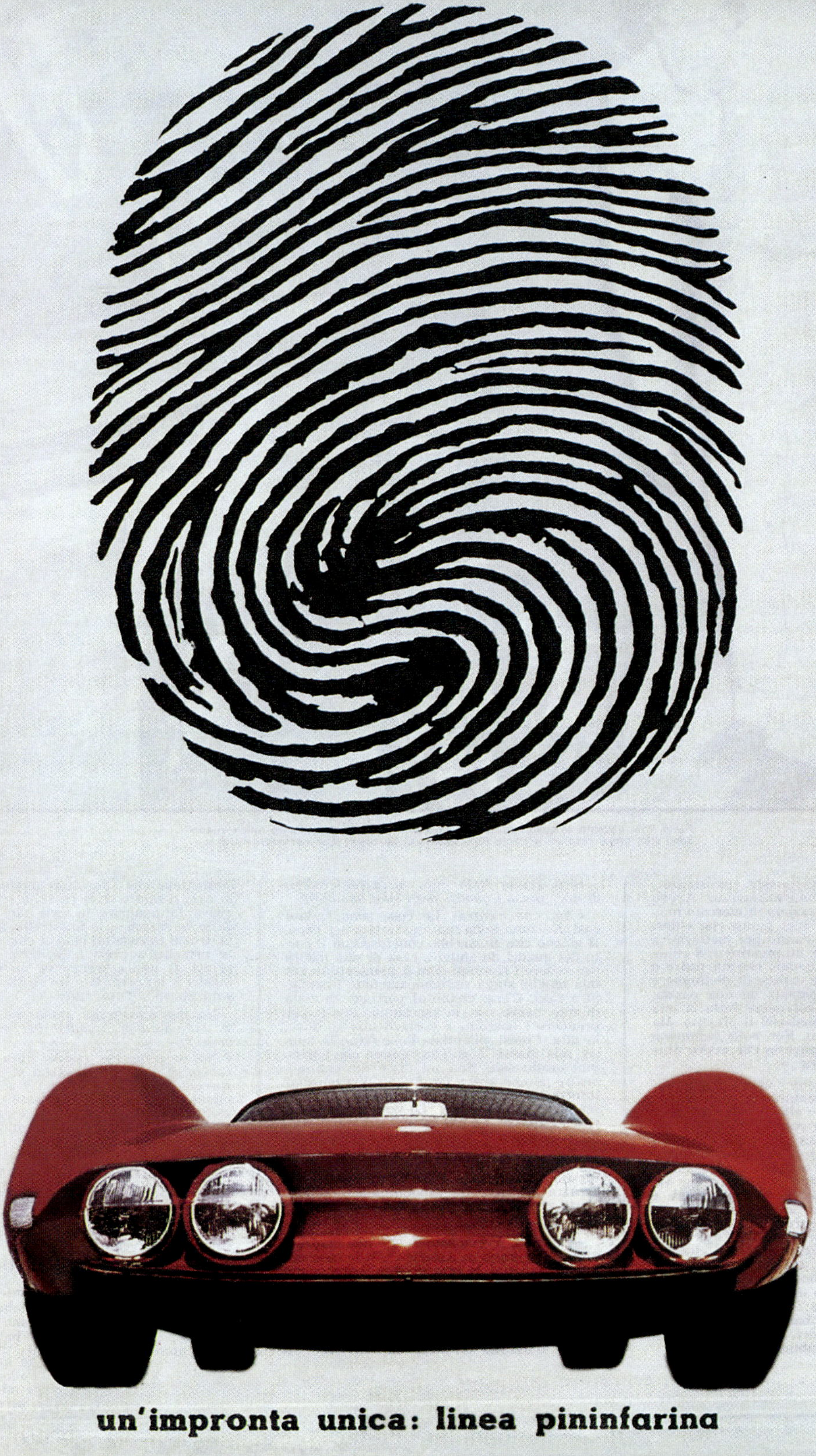

un'impronta unica: linea pininfarina

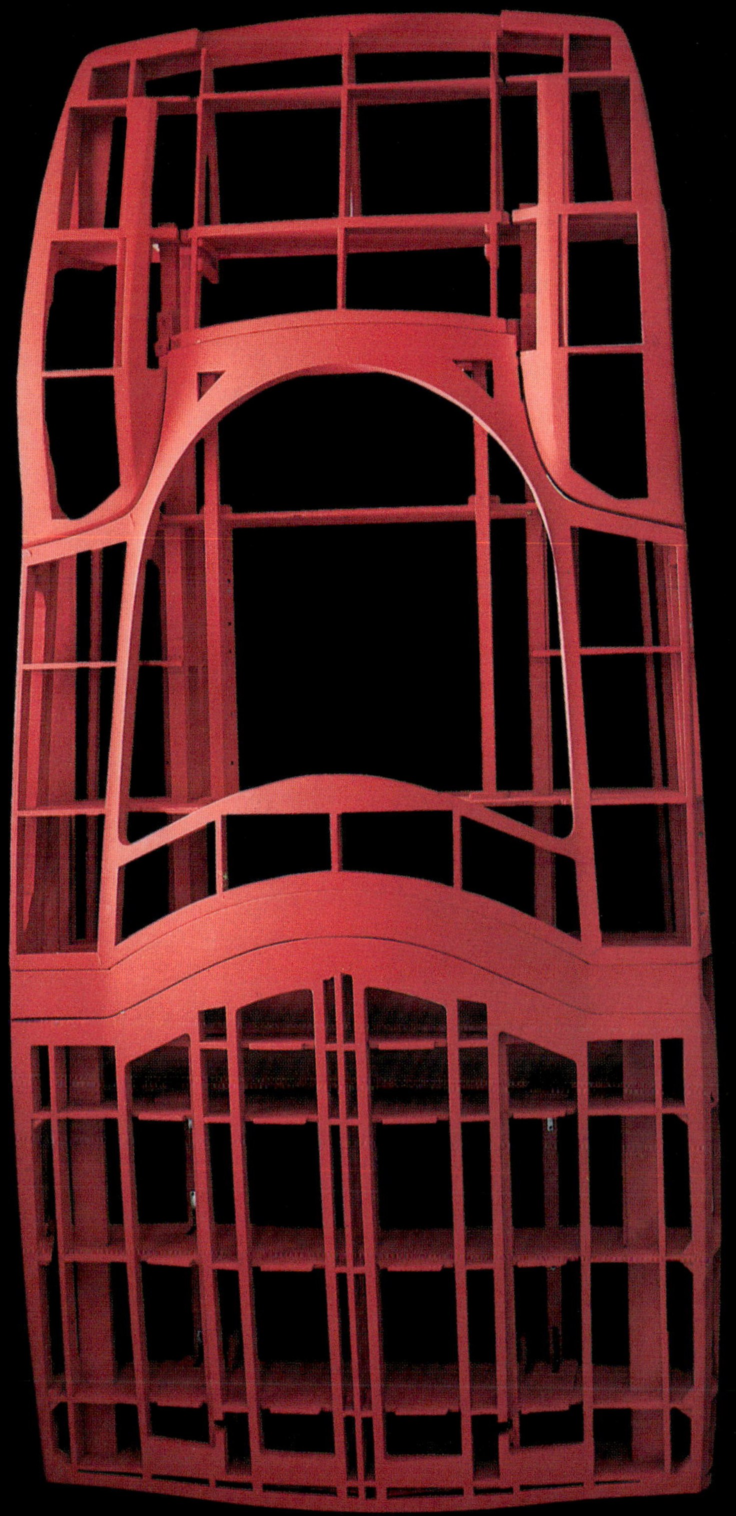

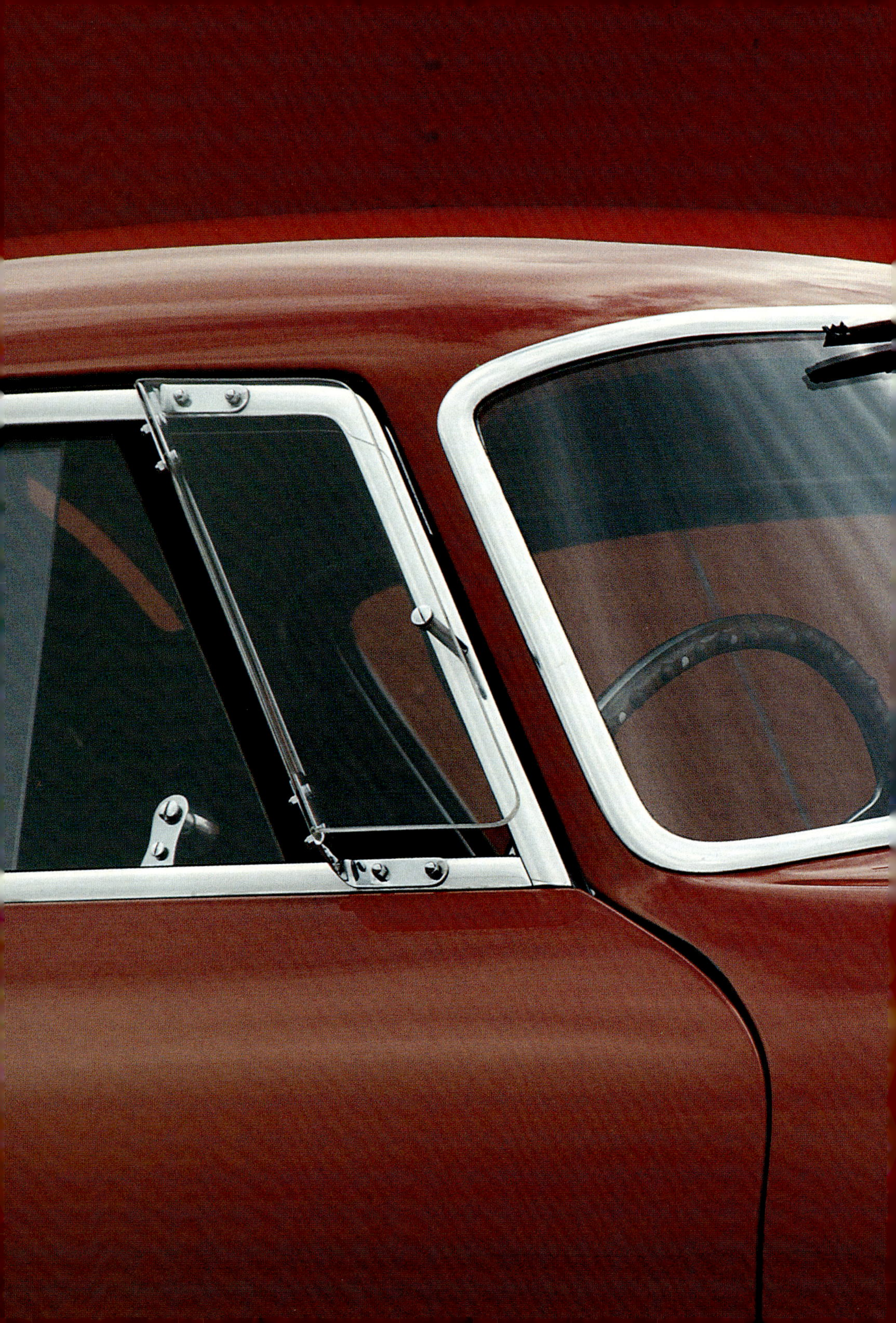

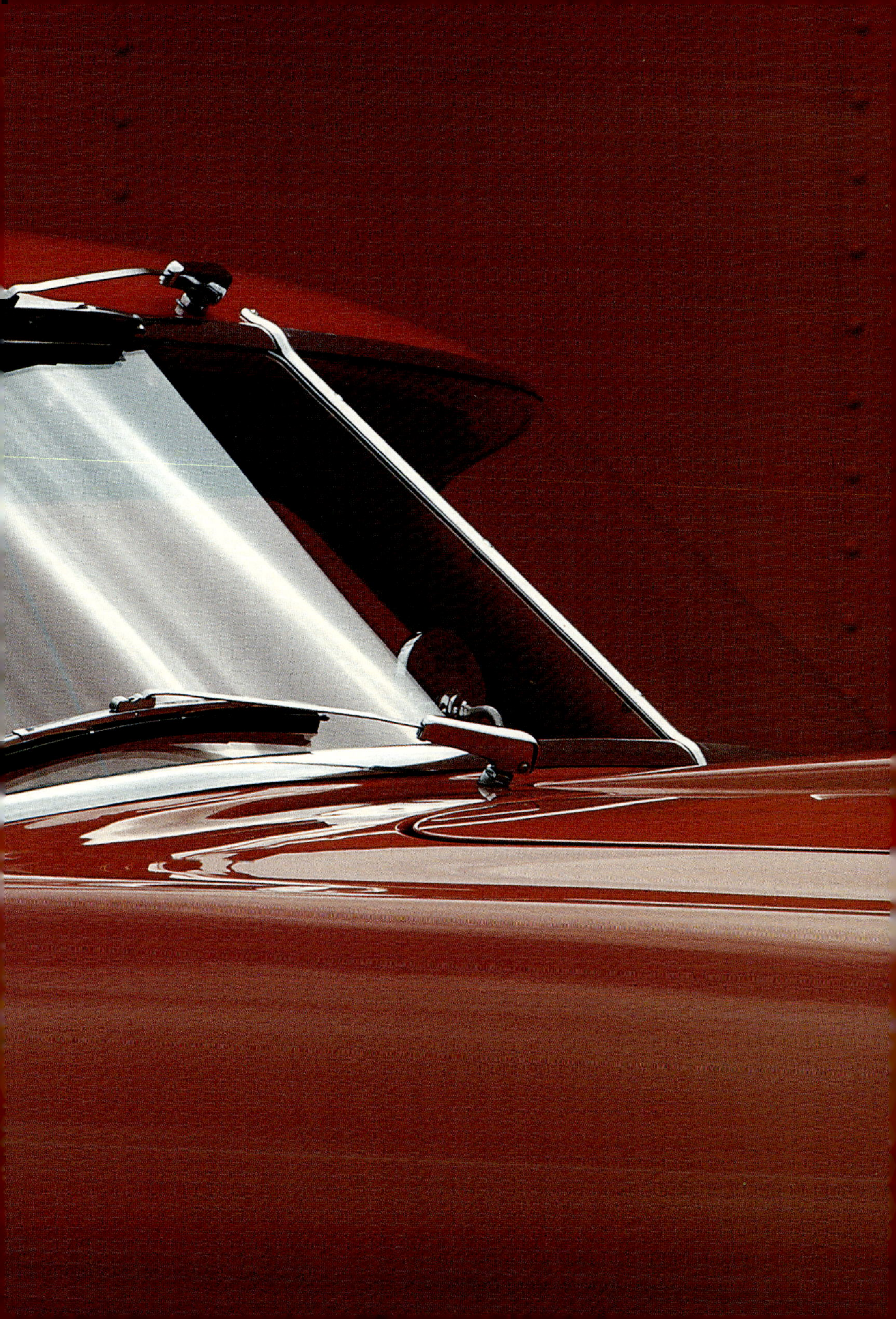

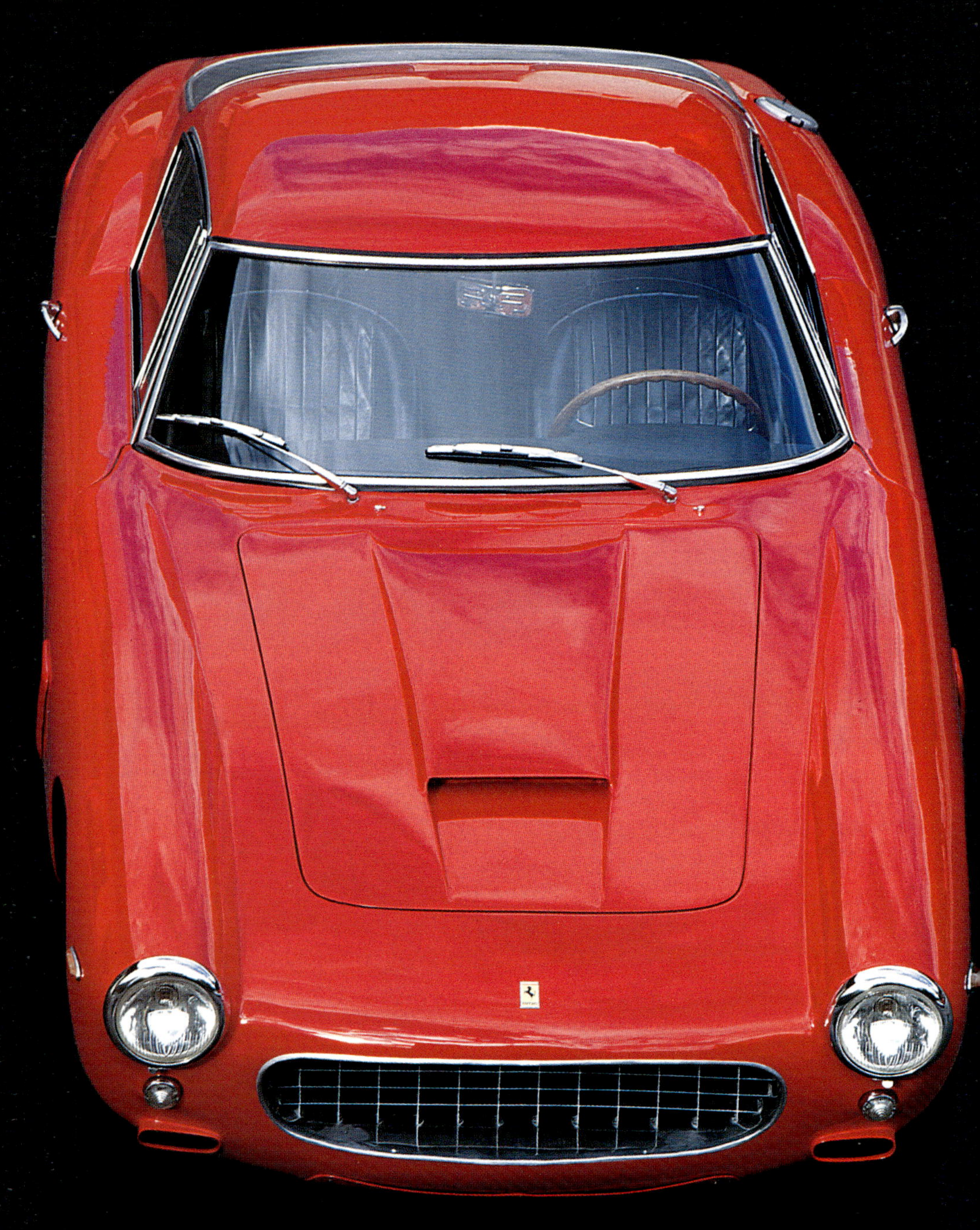

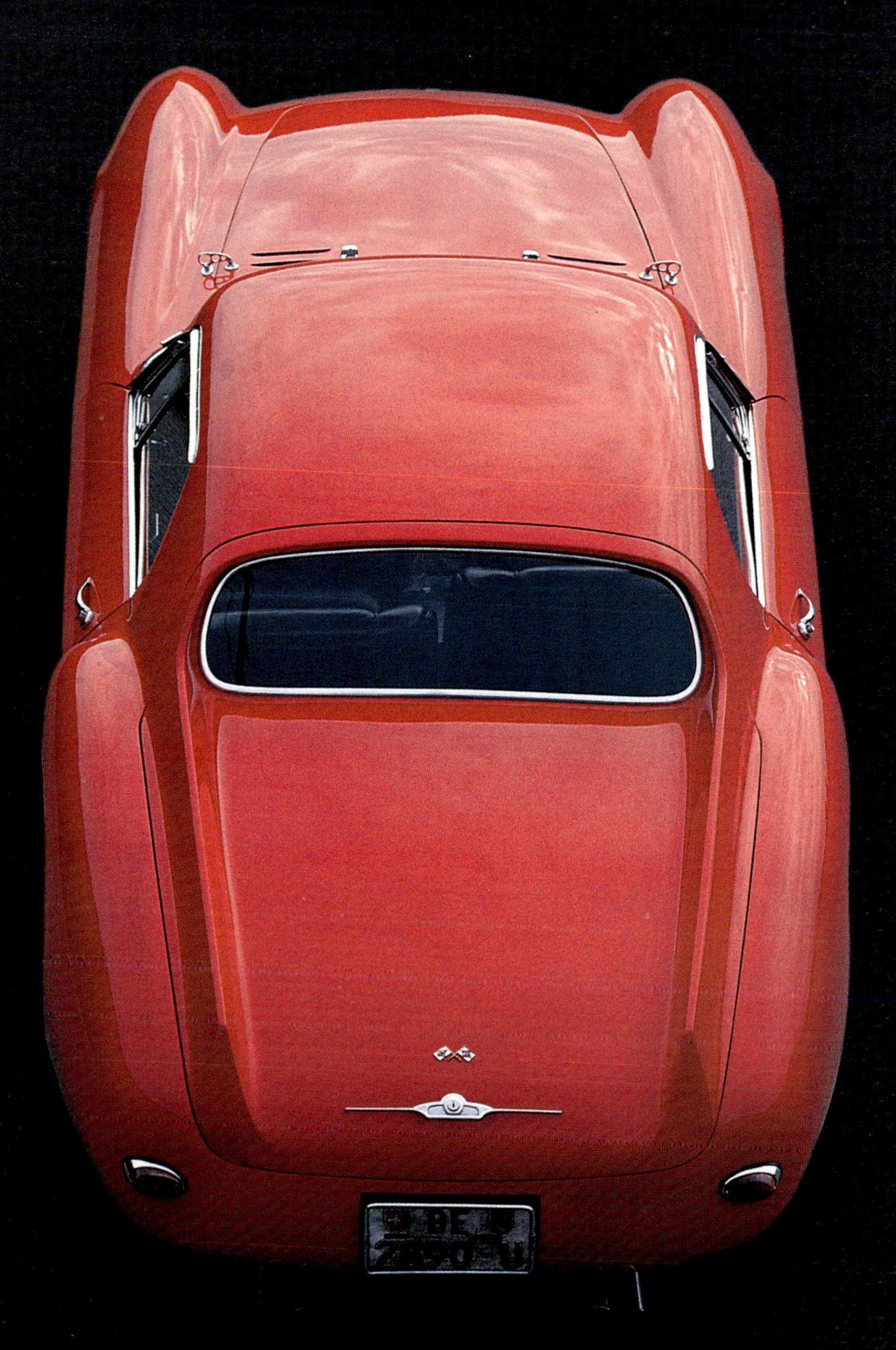
BE

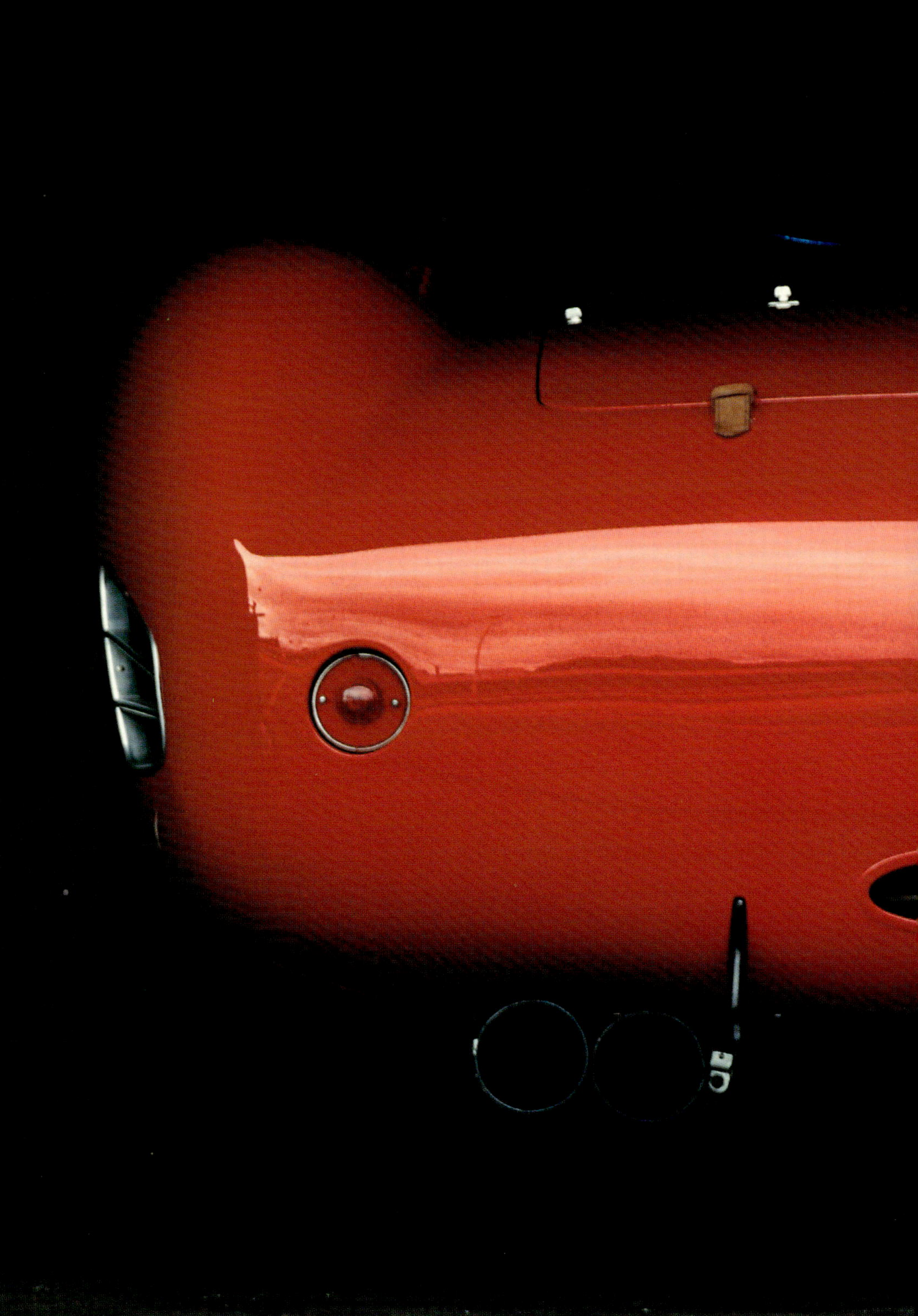

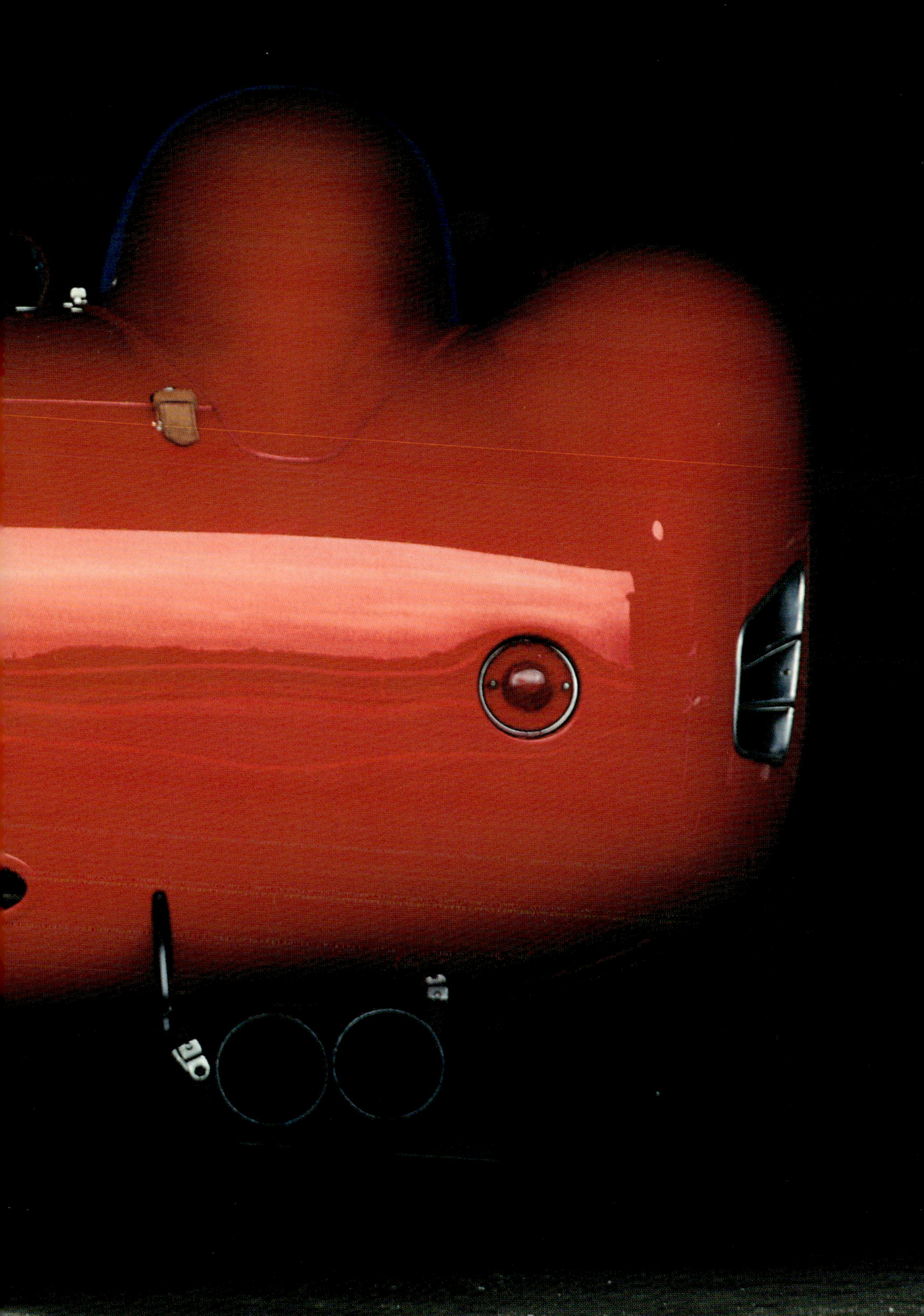

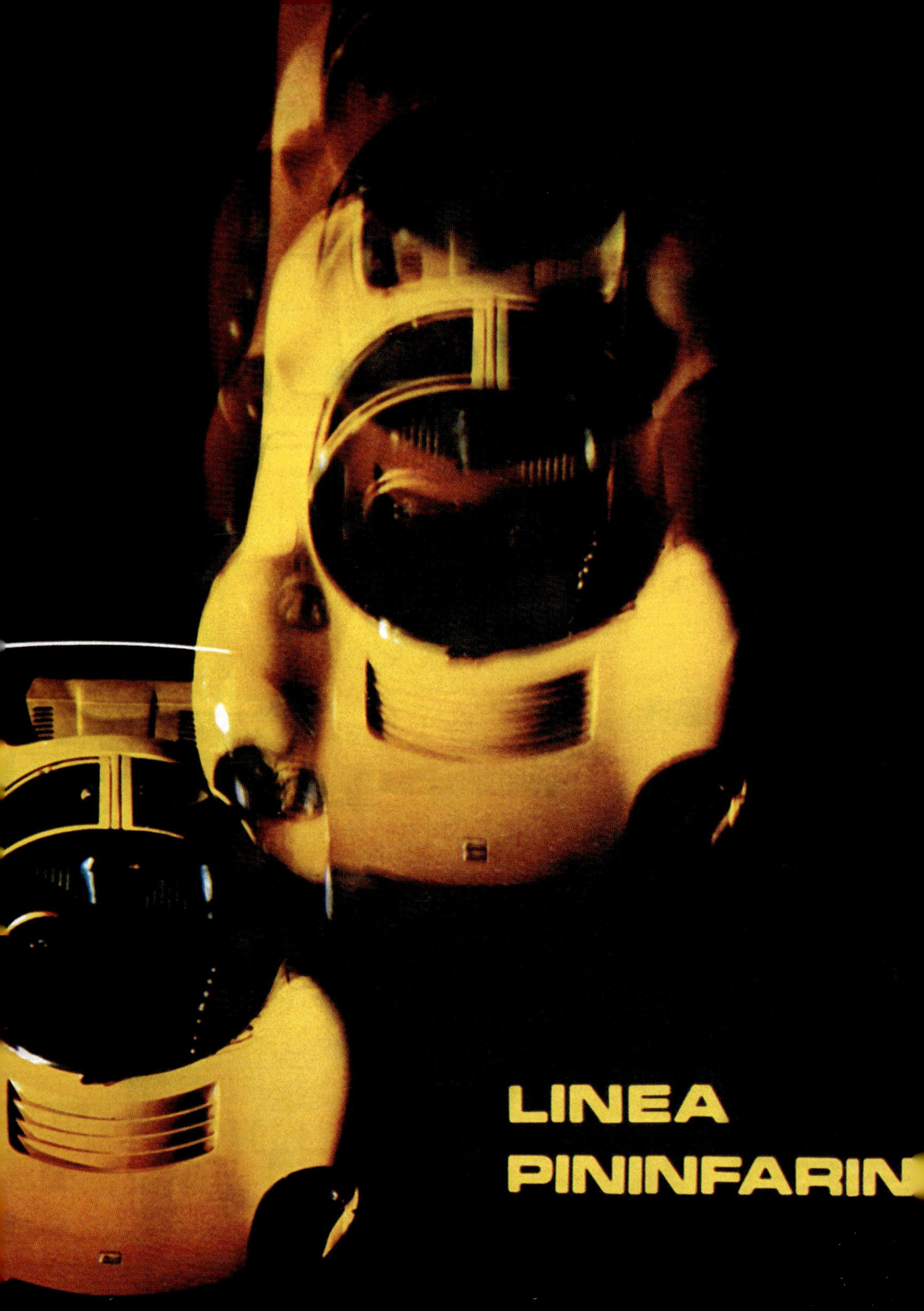
LINEA
PININFARIN

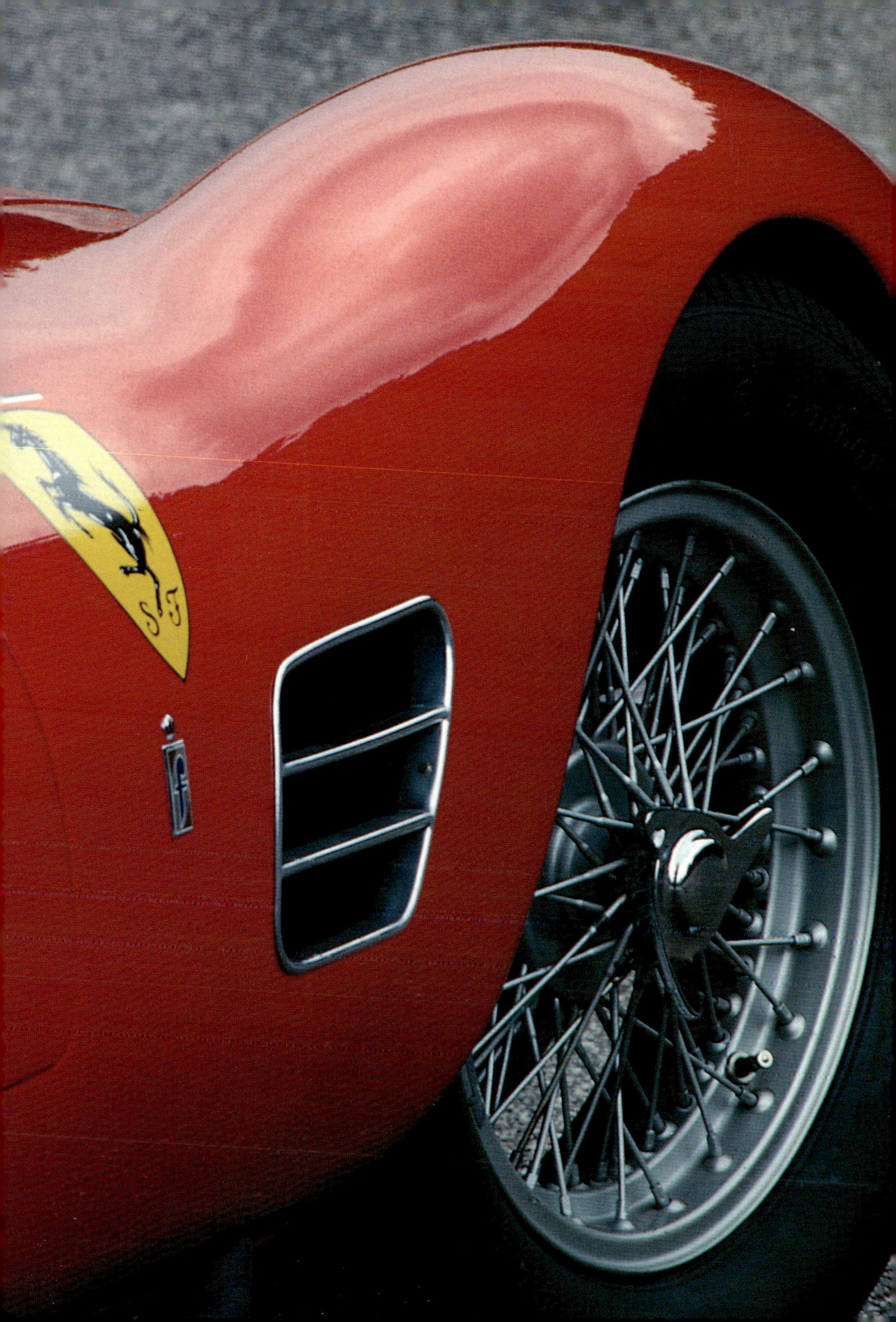

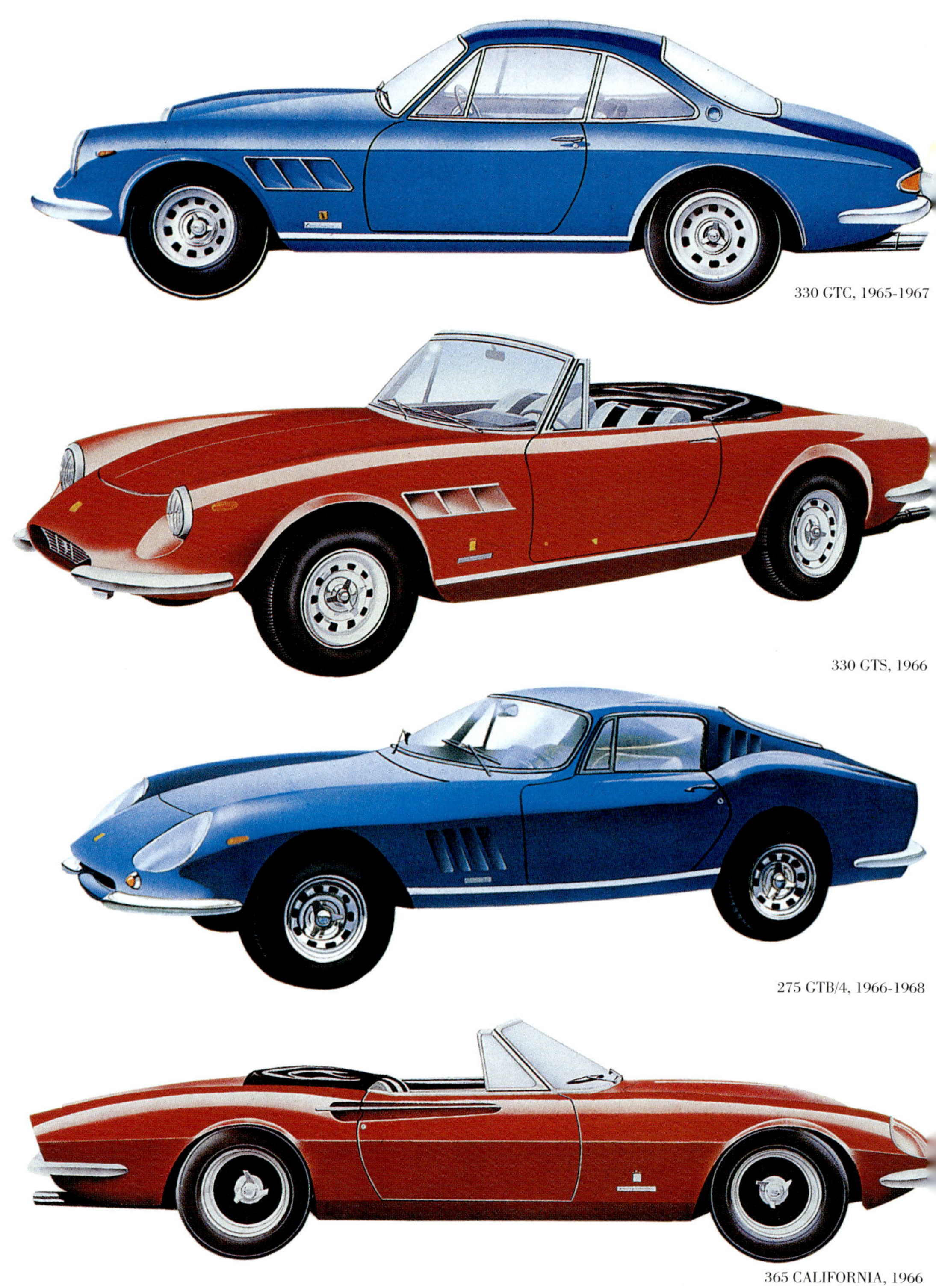

330 GTC, 1965-1967

330 GTS, 1966

275 GTB/4, 1966-1968

365 CALIFORNIA, 1966

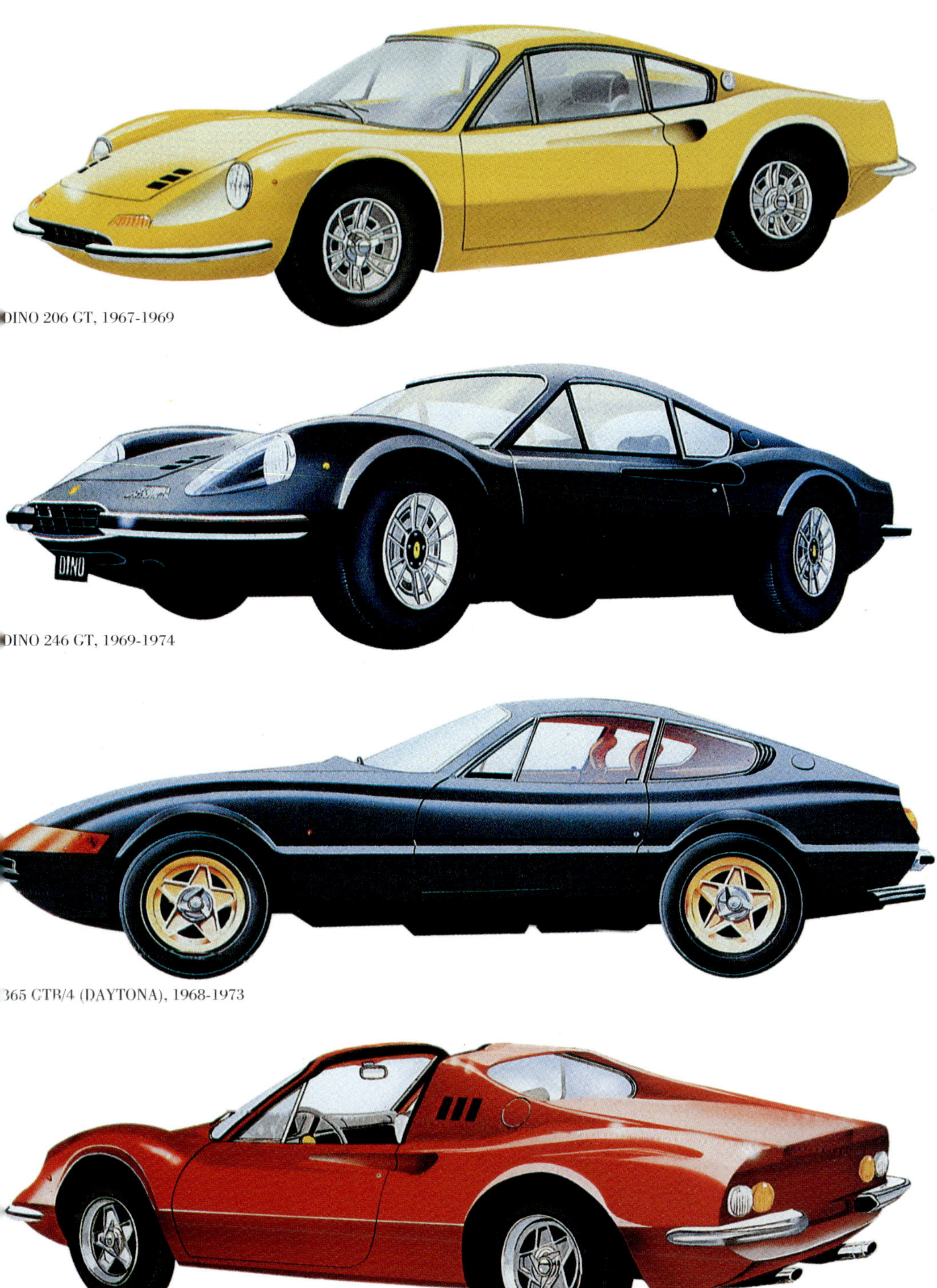

DINO 206 GT, 1967-1969

DINO 246 GT, 1969-1974

365 GTB/4 (DAYTONA), 1968-1973

DINO 246 GTS, 1972-1974

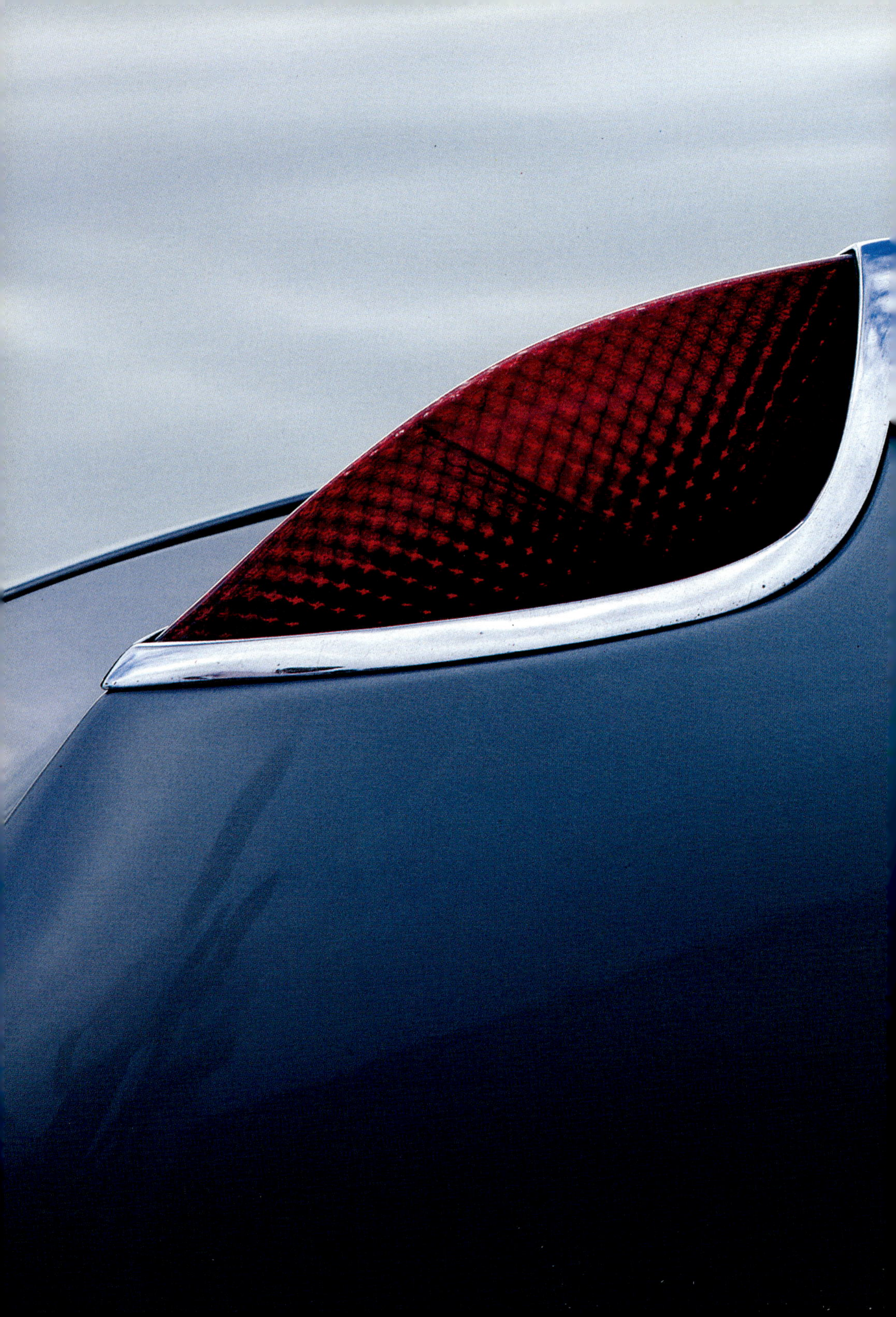

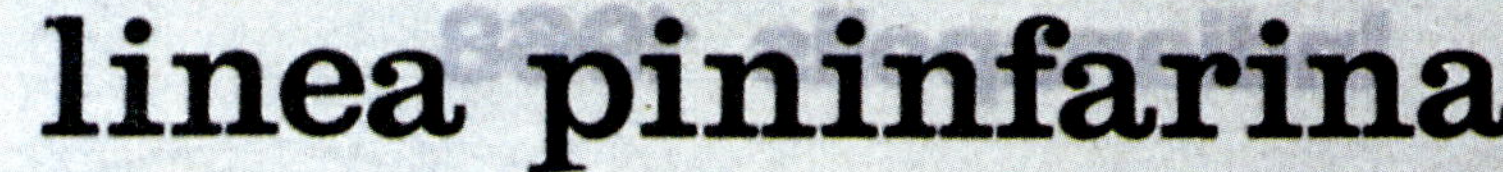
linea pininfarina

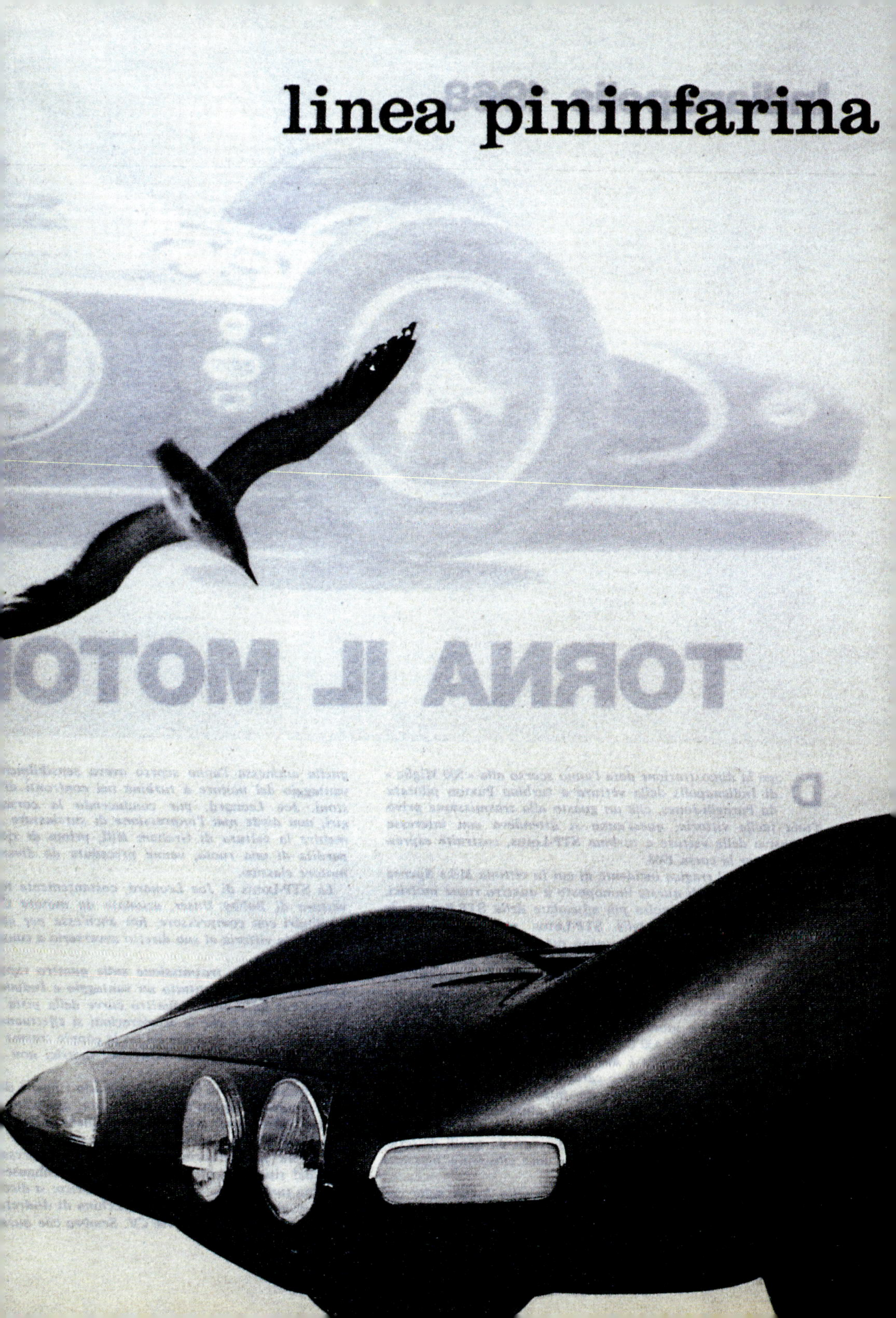

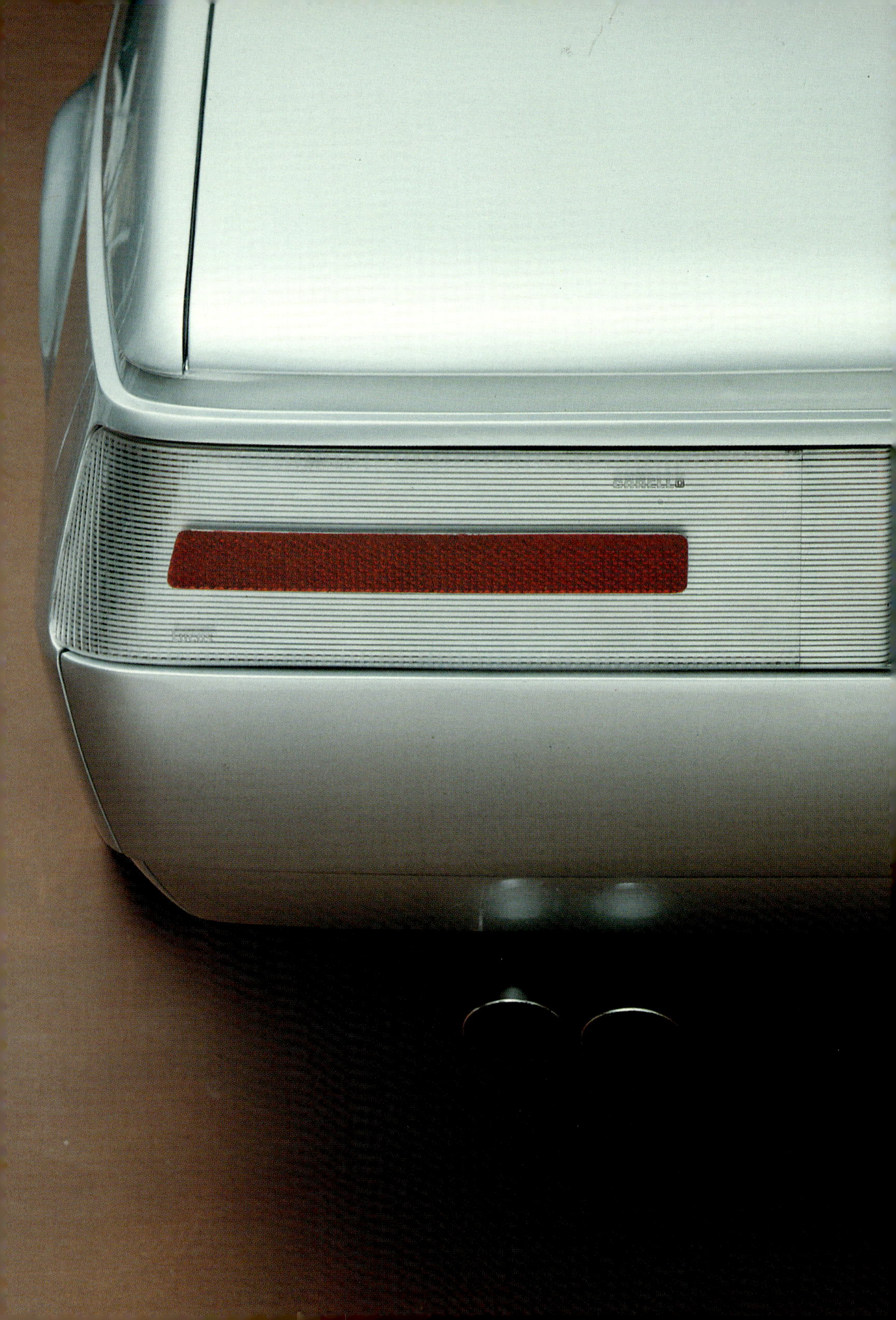

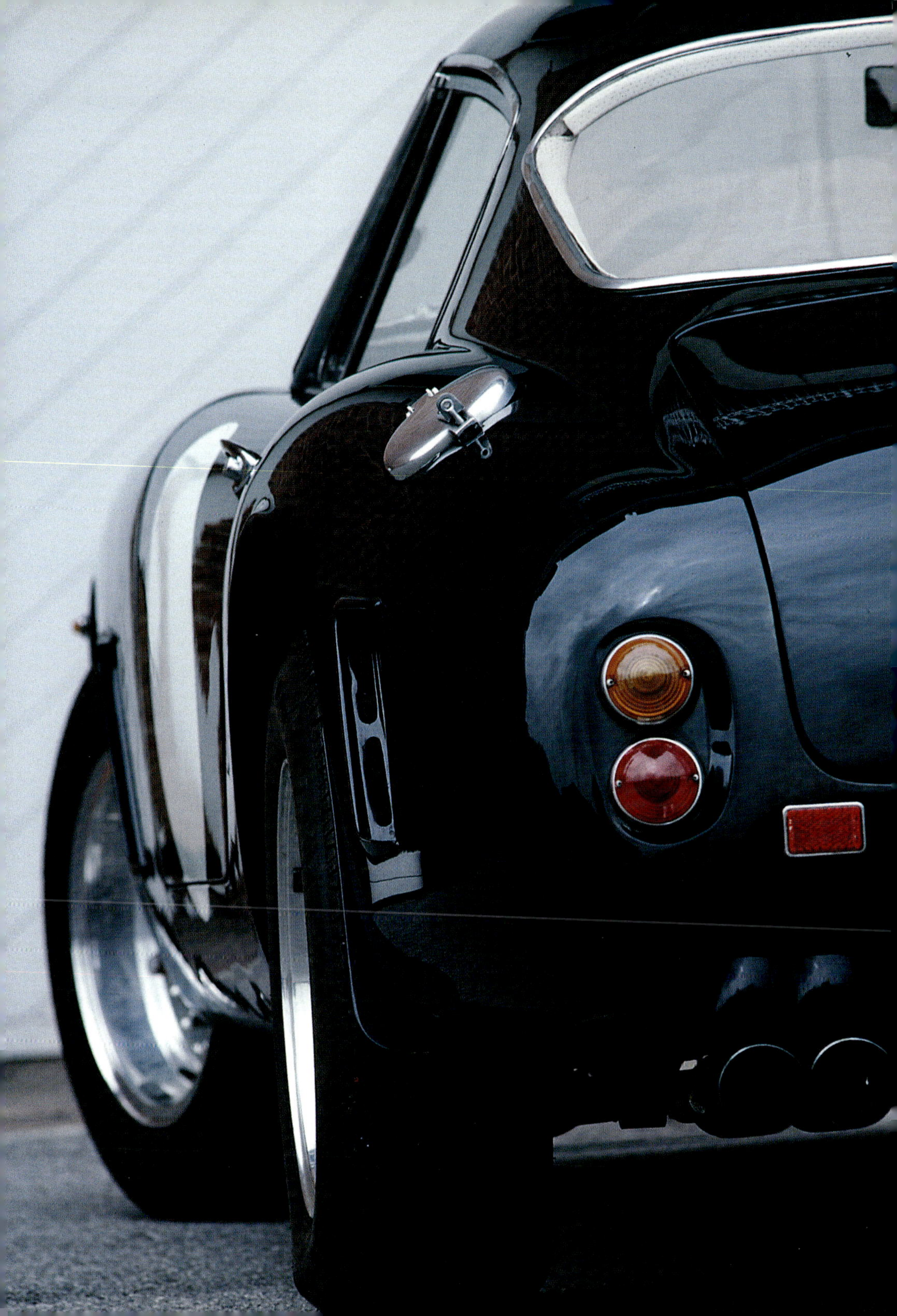

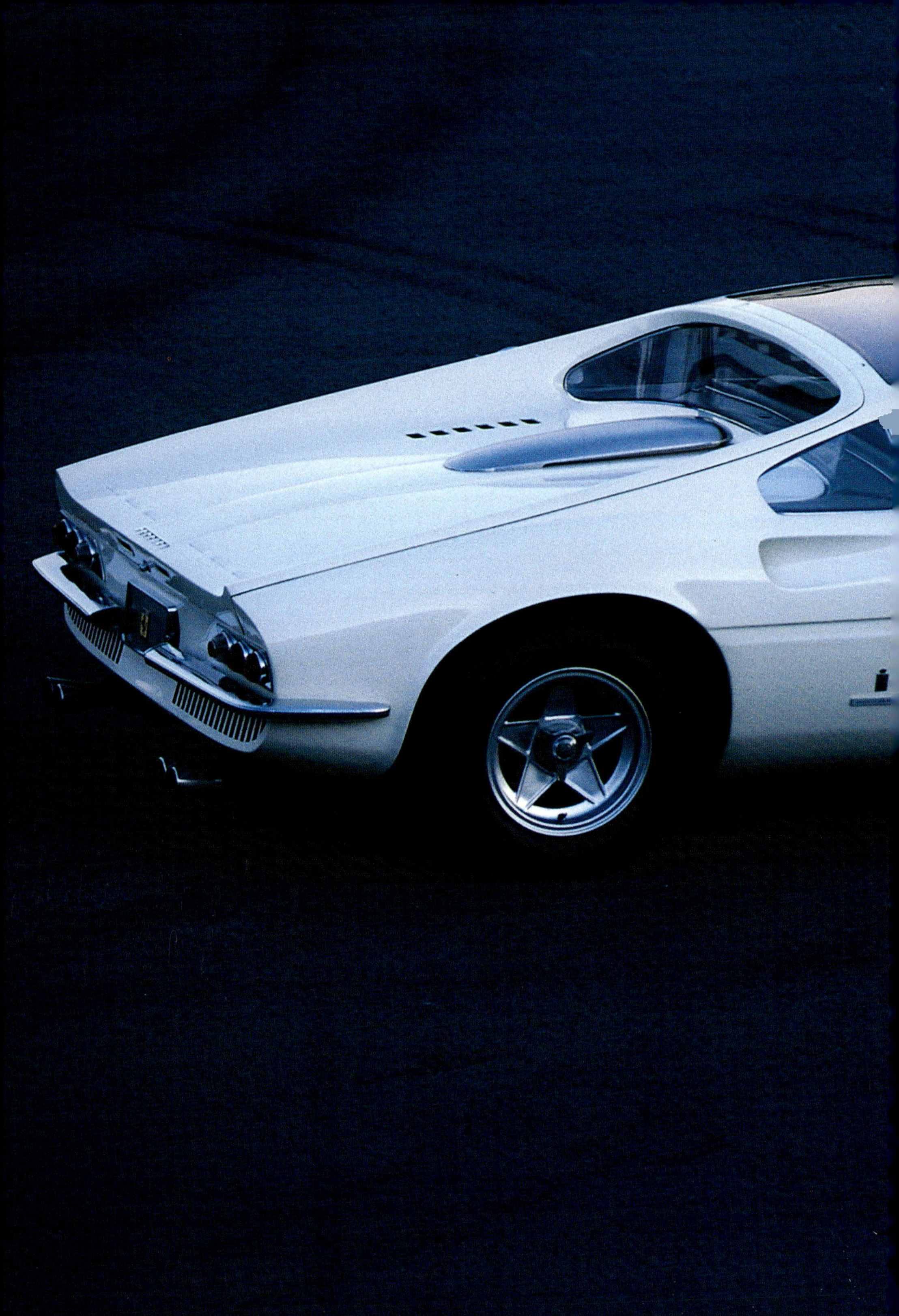

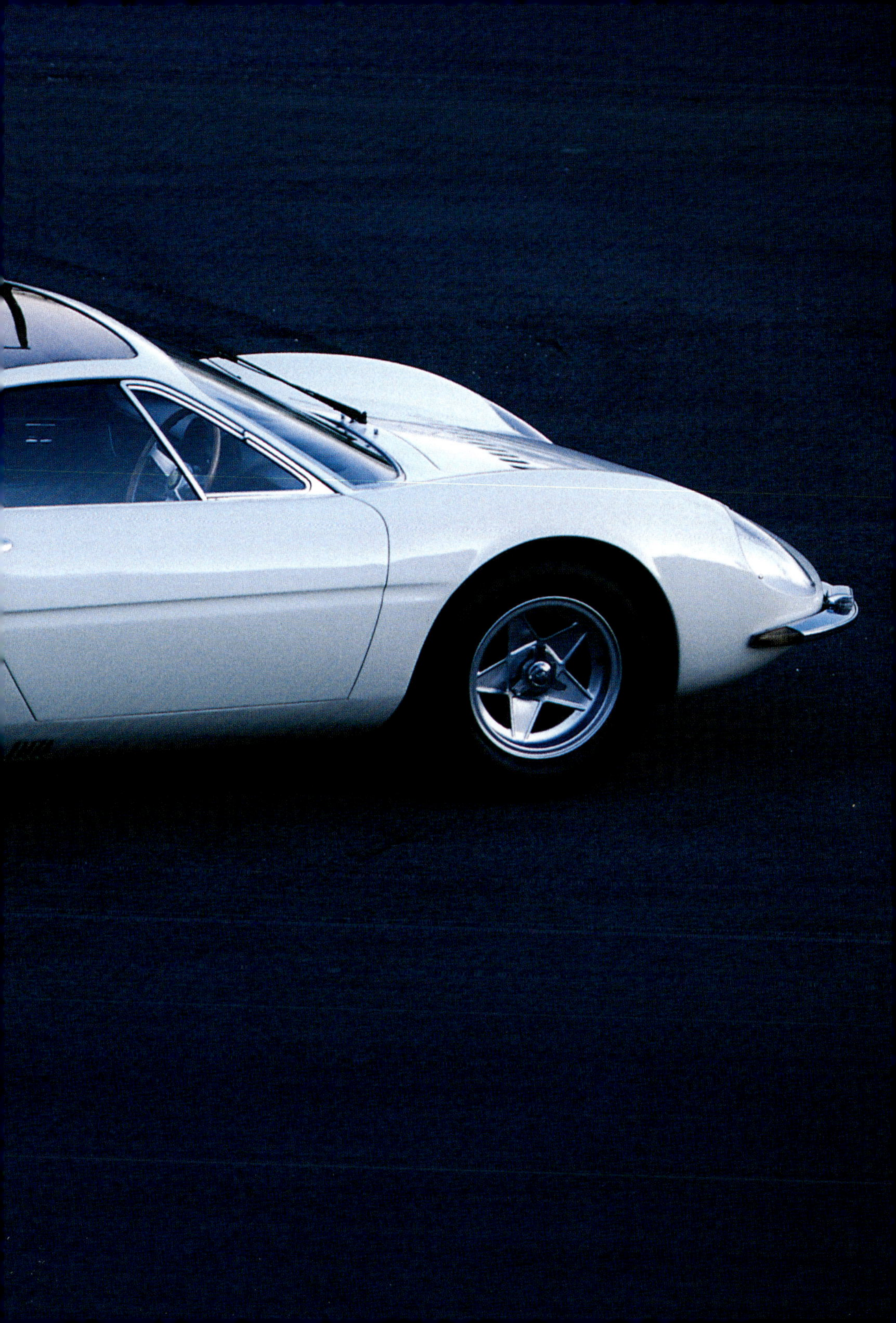

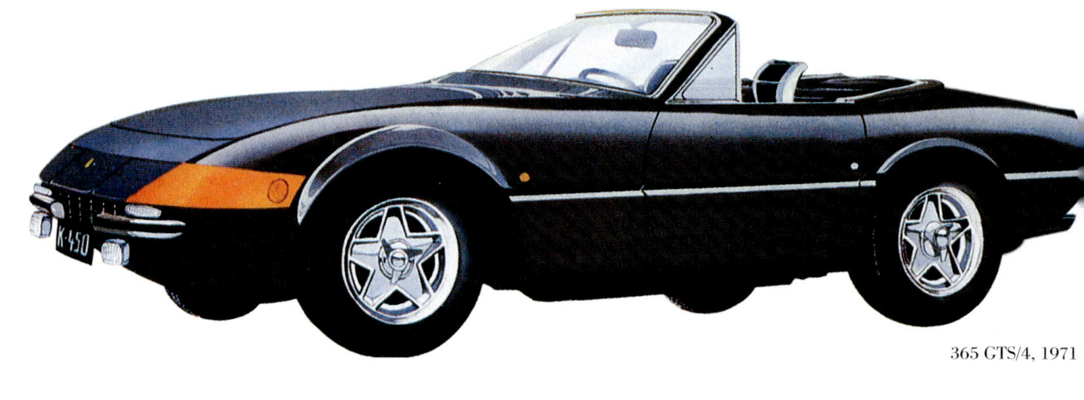

365 GTS/4, 1971

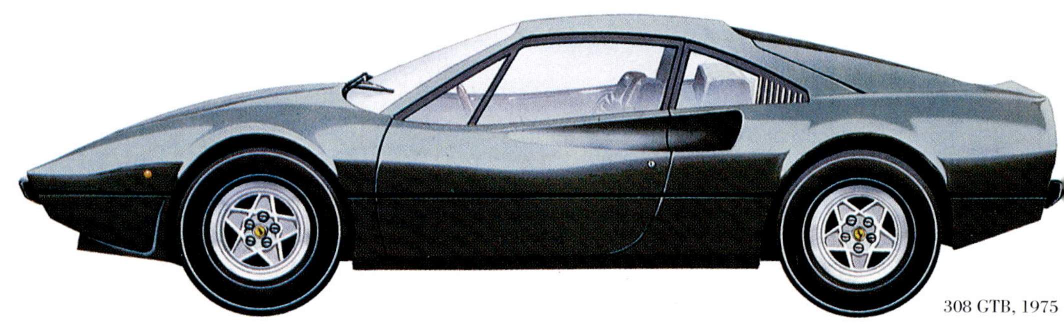

308 GTB, 1975

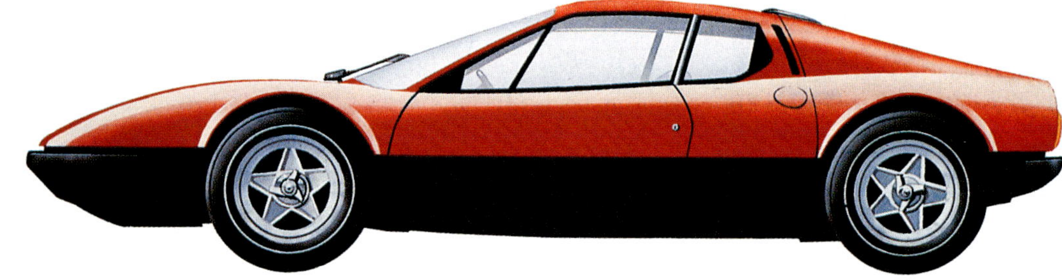

365 BB (BOXER), 1973-1976

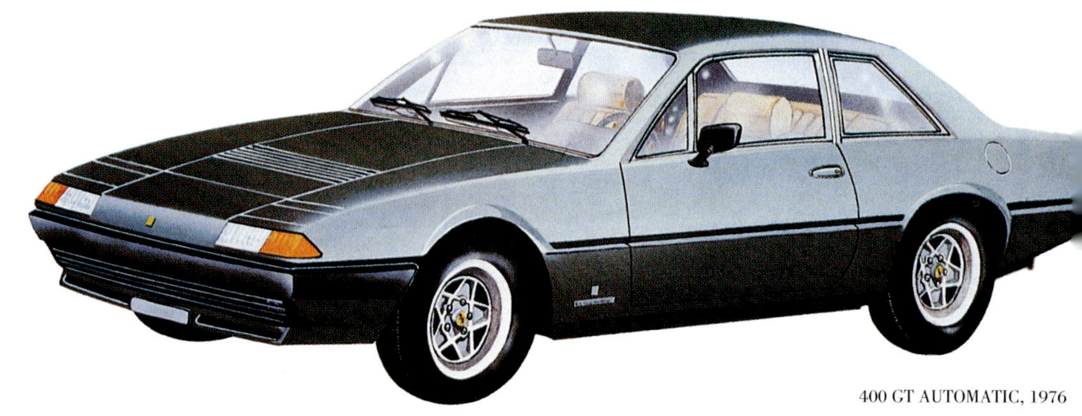

400 GT AUTOMATIC, 1976

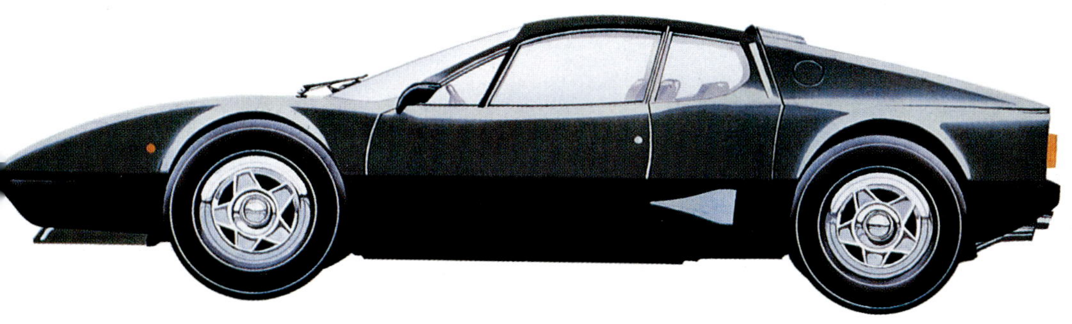

BB 512 (BERLINETTA BOXER), 1976

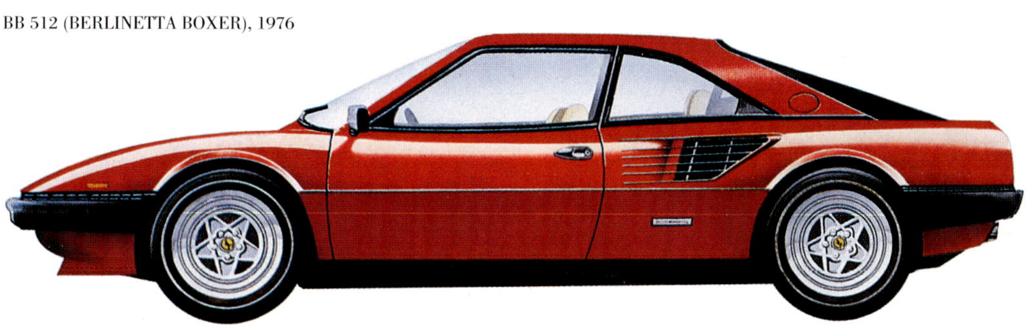

308 GTS, 1977

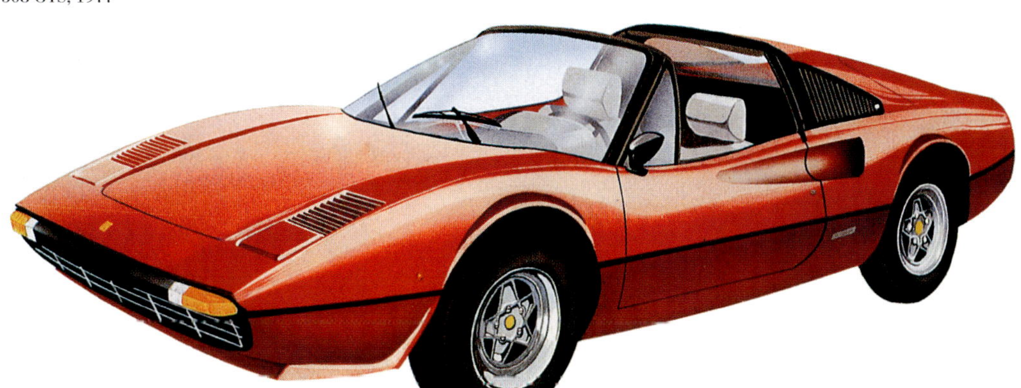

MONDIAL 8, 1980

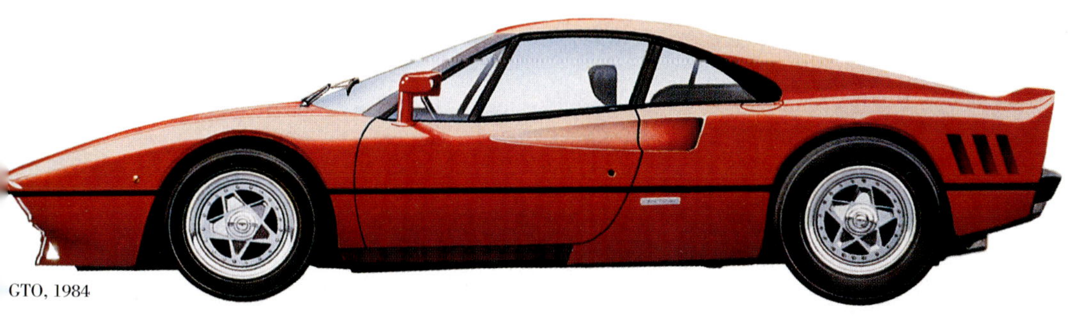

GTO, 1984

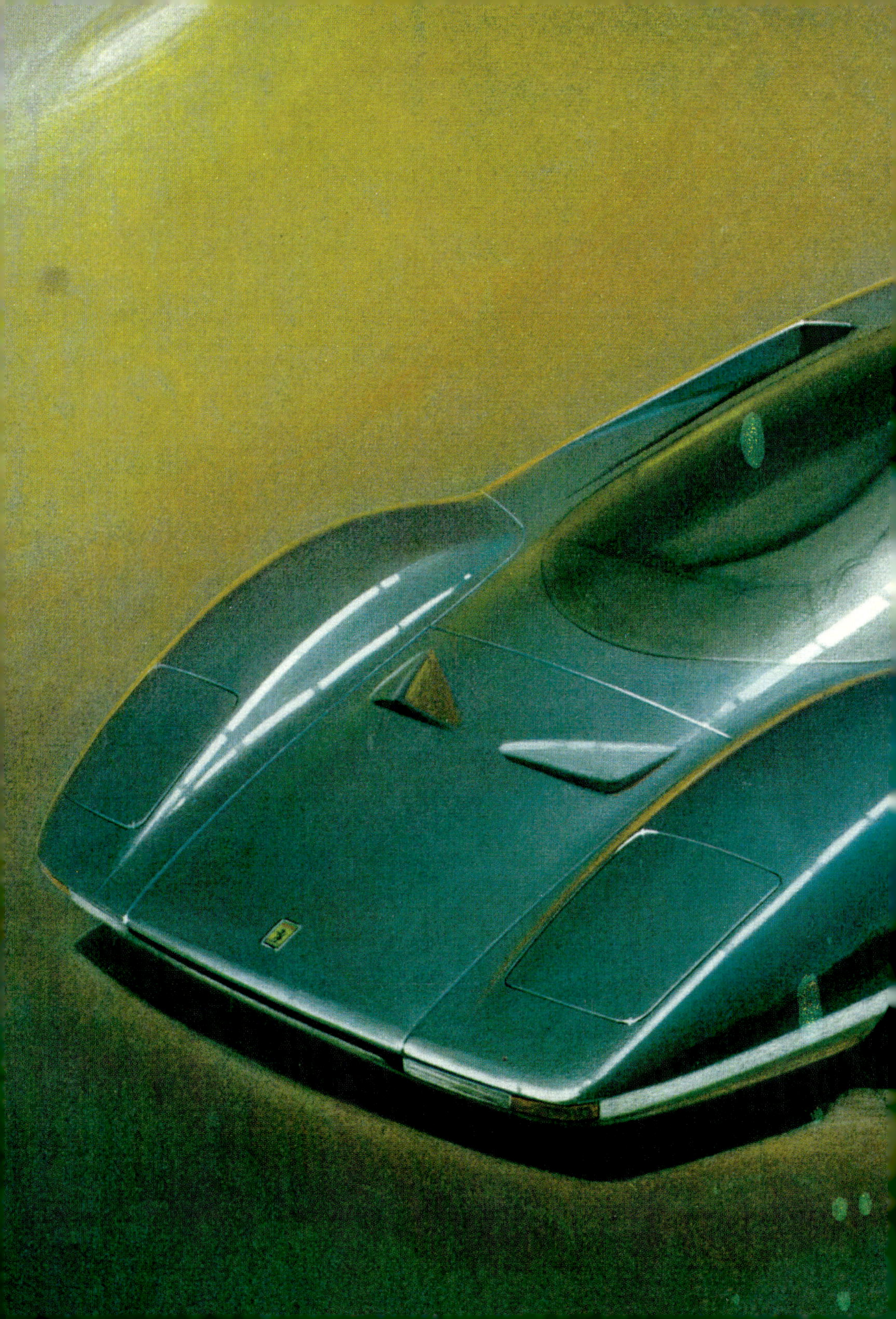

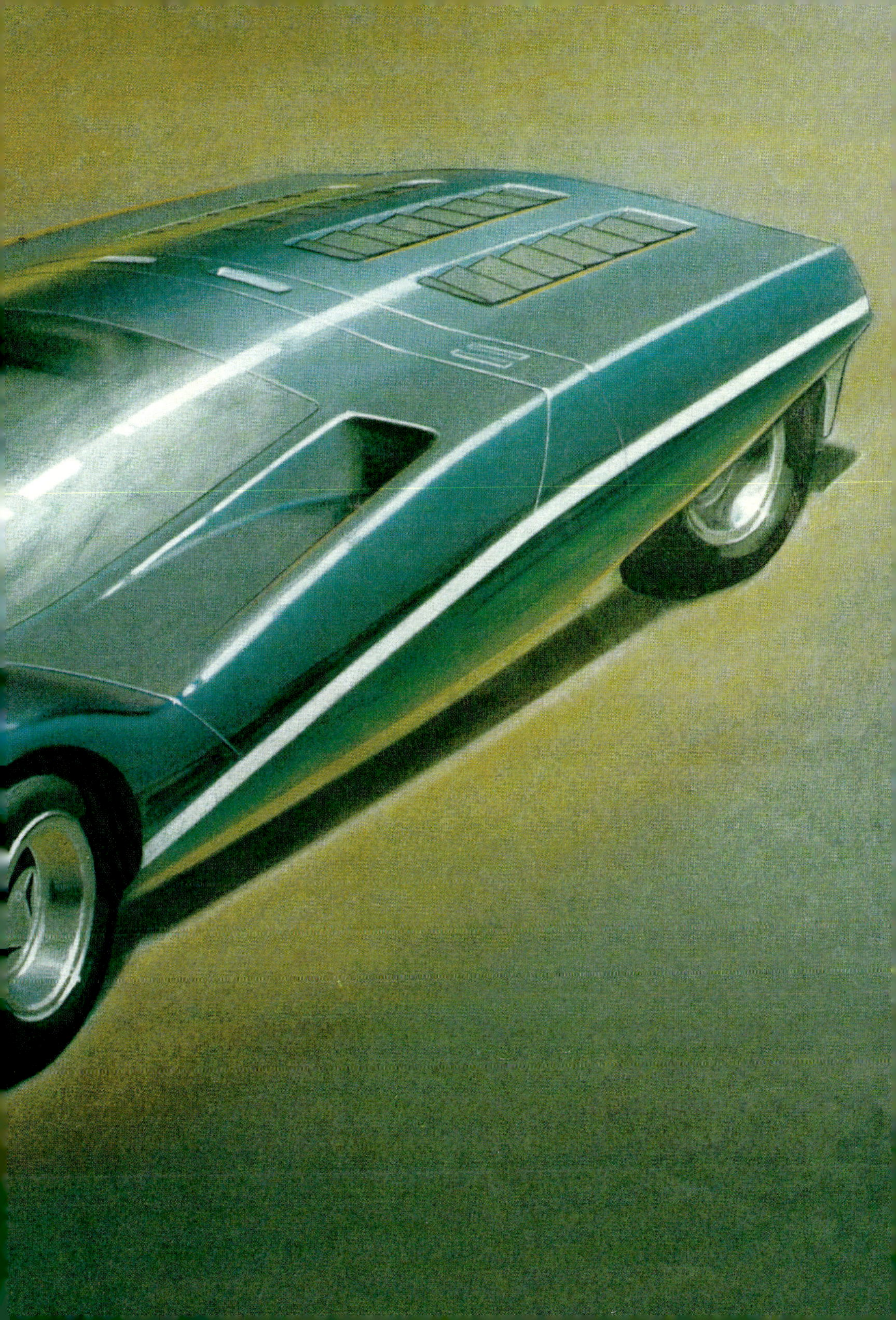

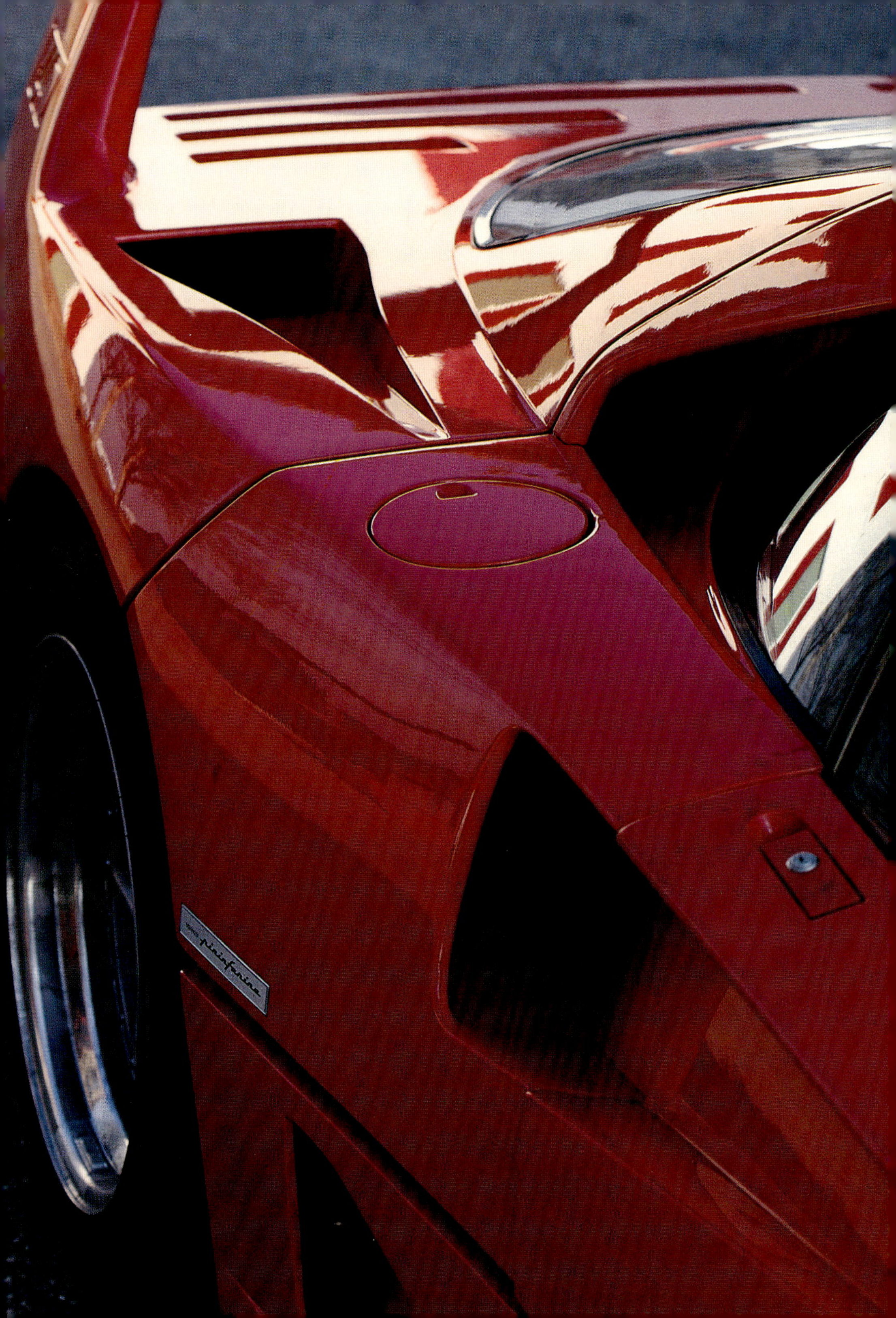
pininfarina

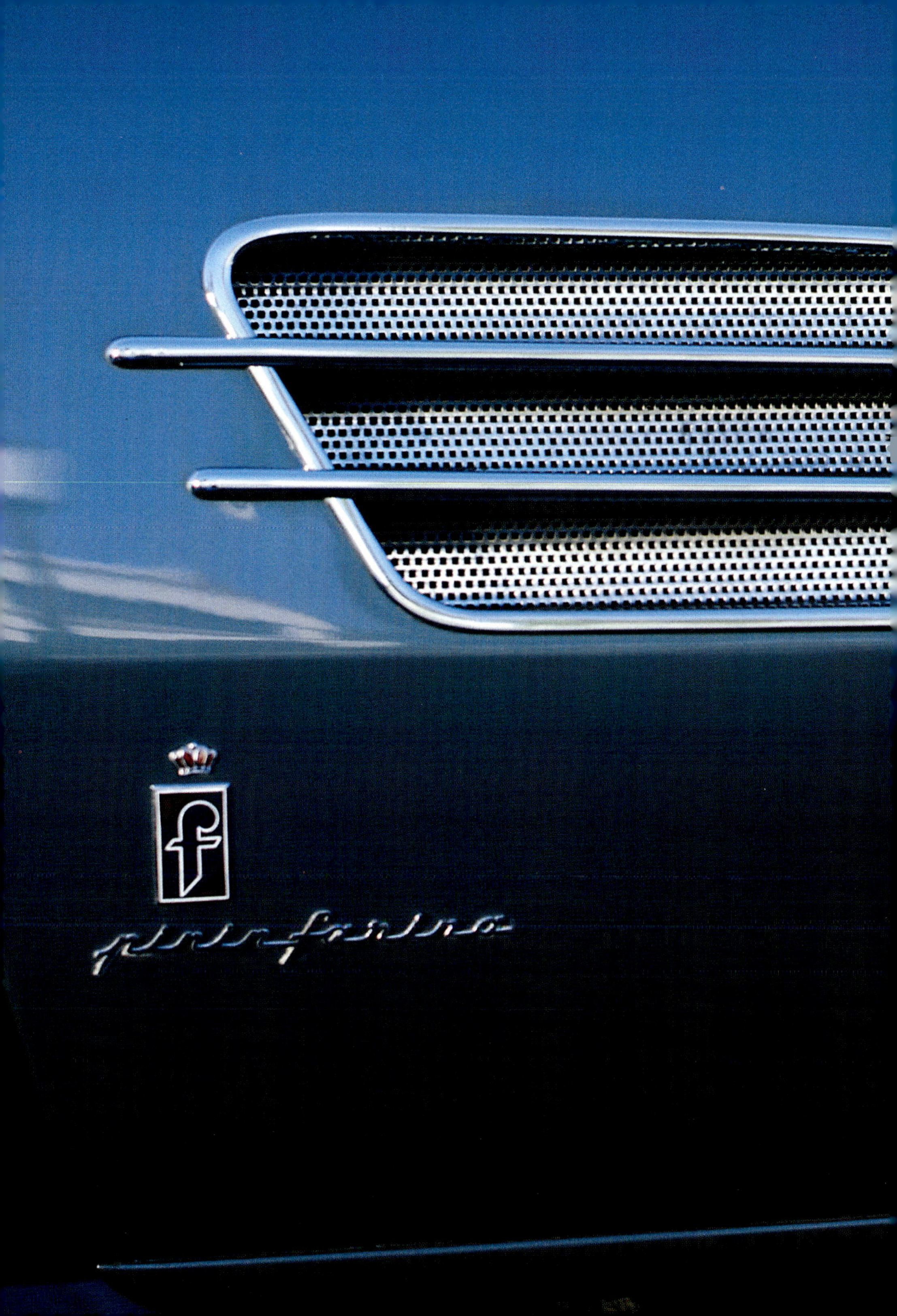
pininfarina

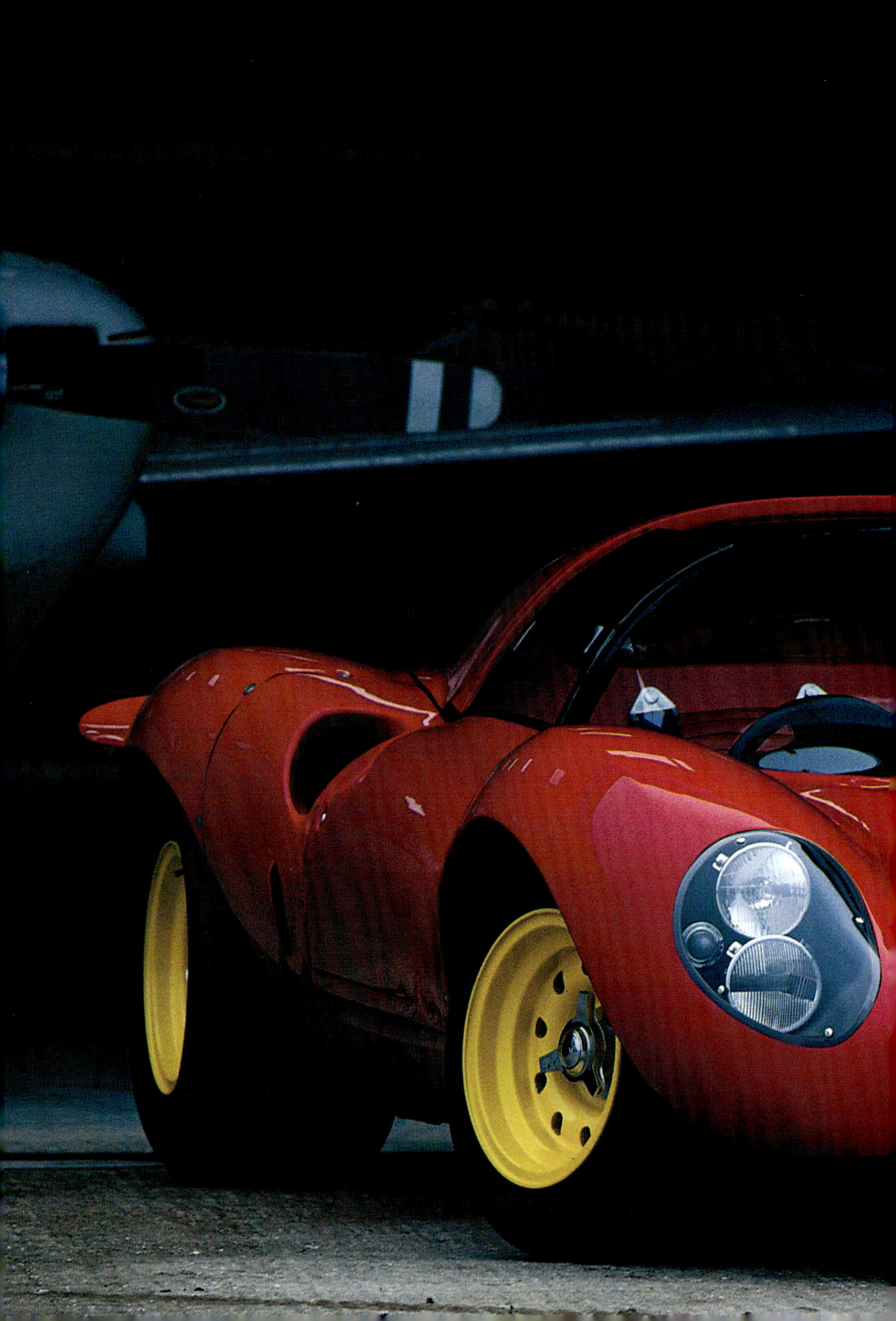

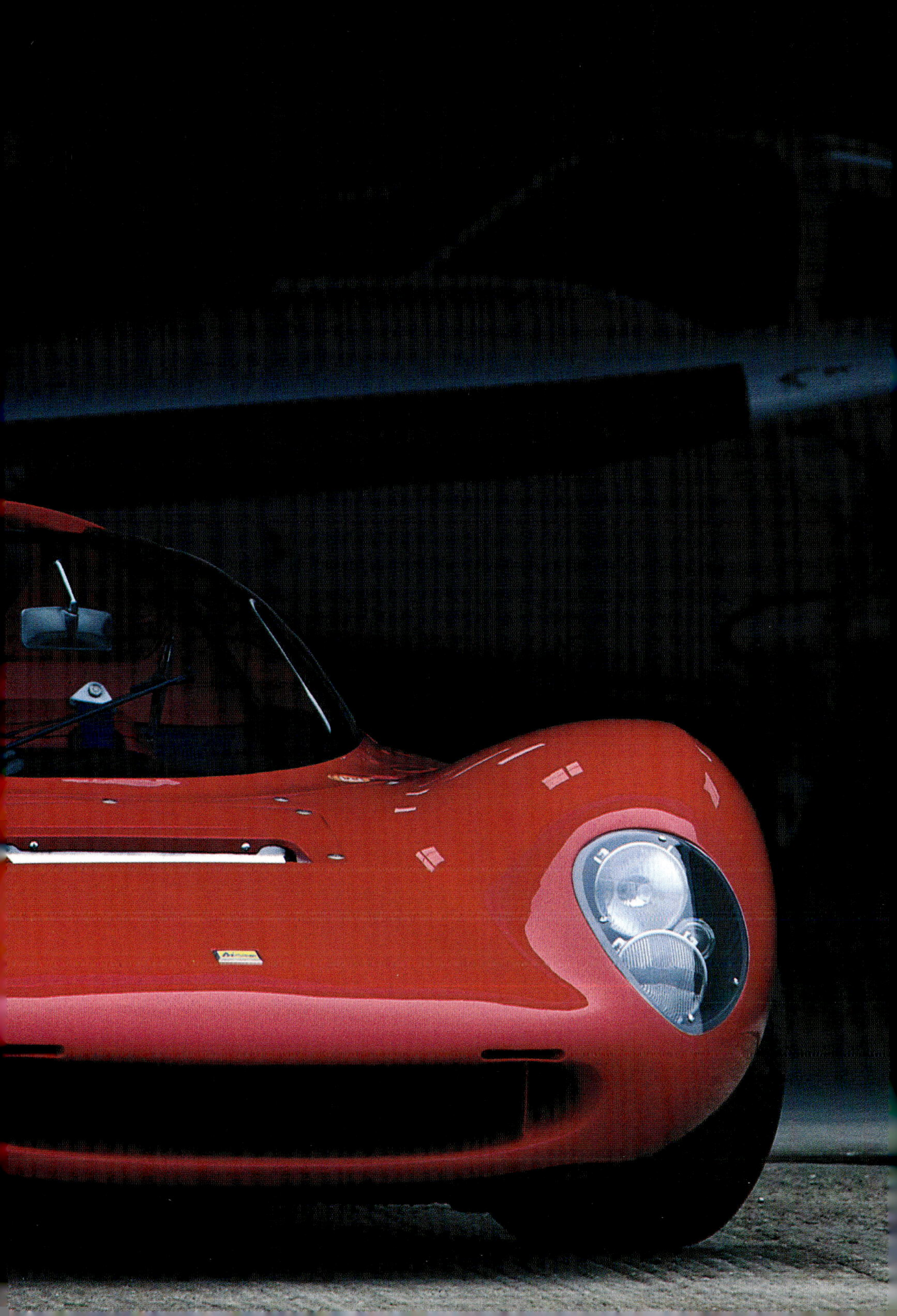

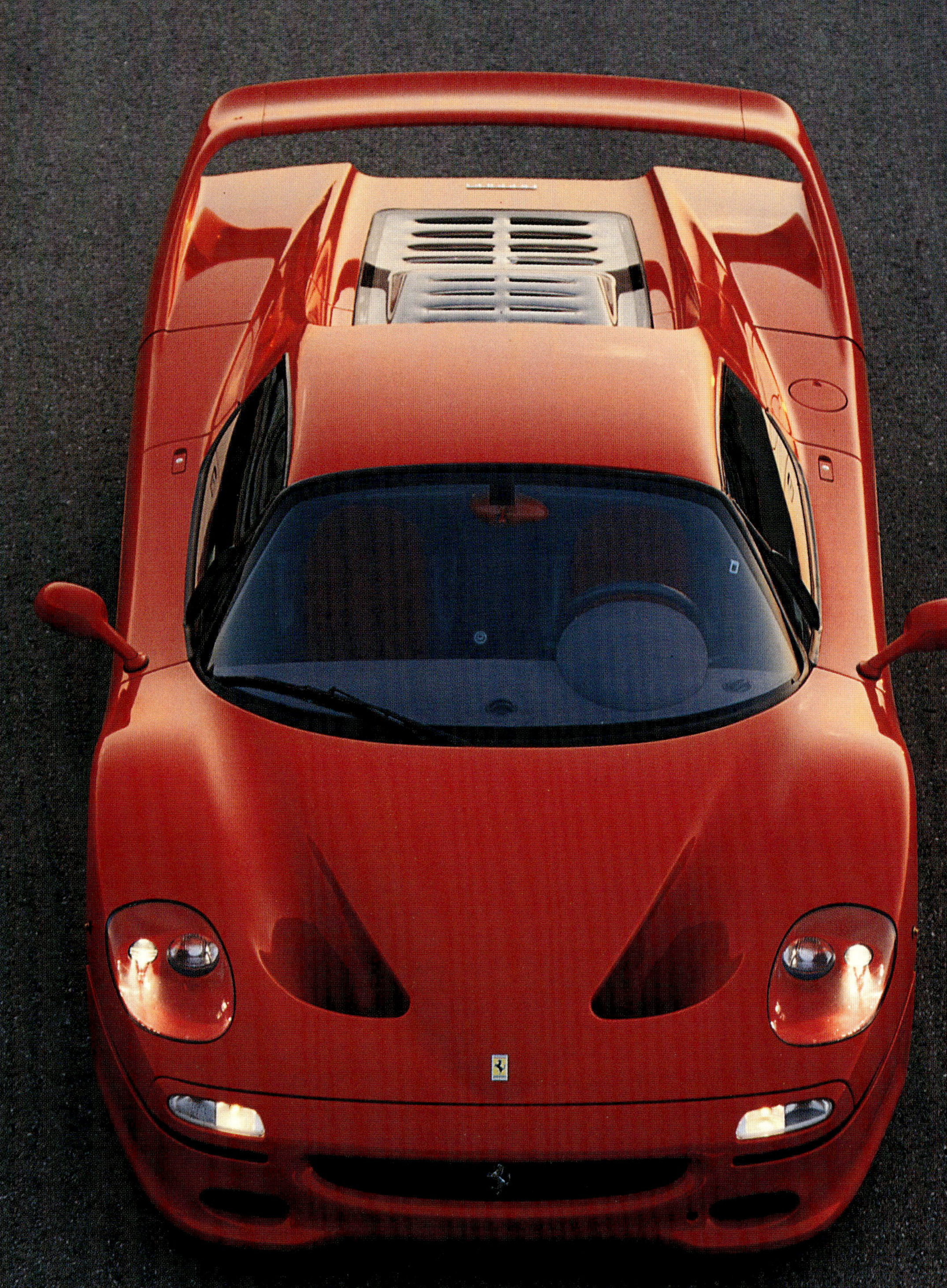

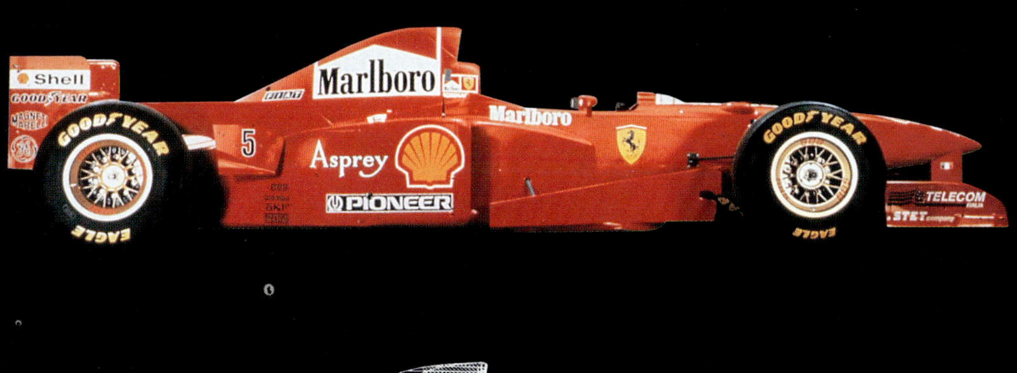
Shell
GOODYEAR
Marlboro
Marlboro
5
Asprey
PIONEER
GOODYEAR
TELECOM
EAGLE
EAGLE

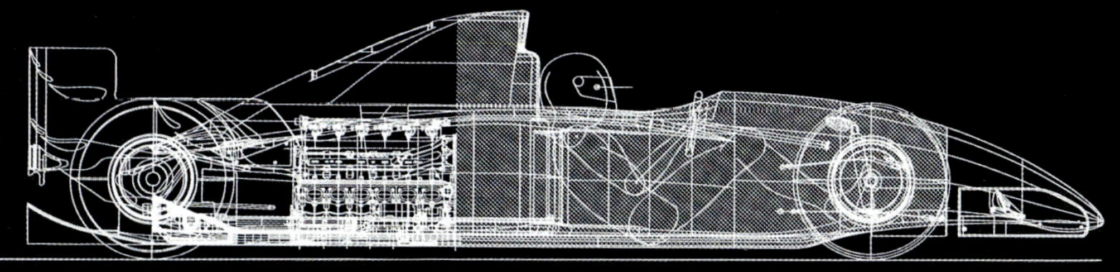

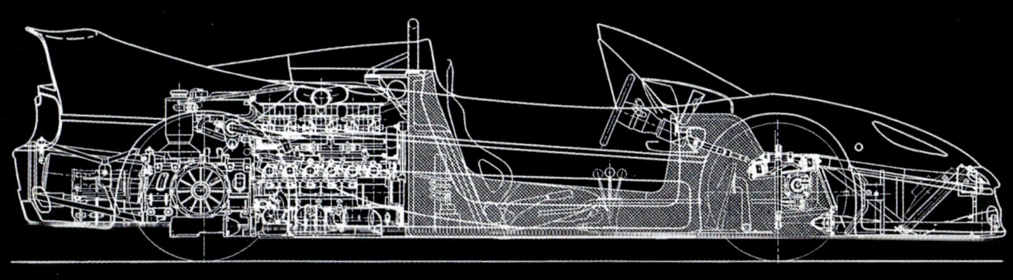

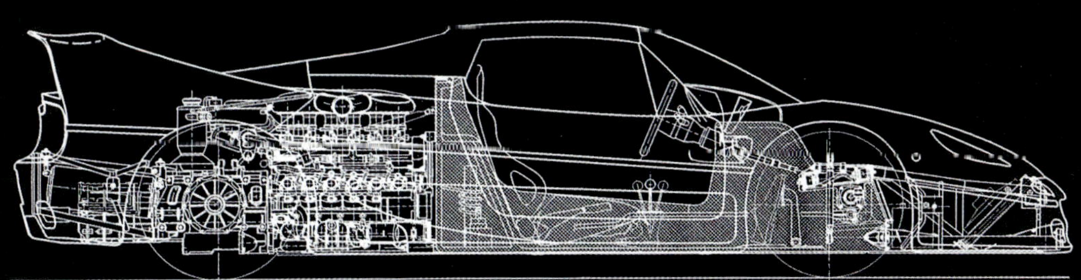

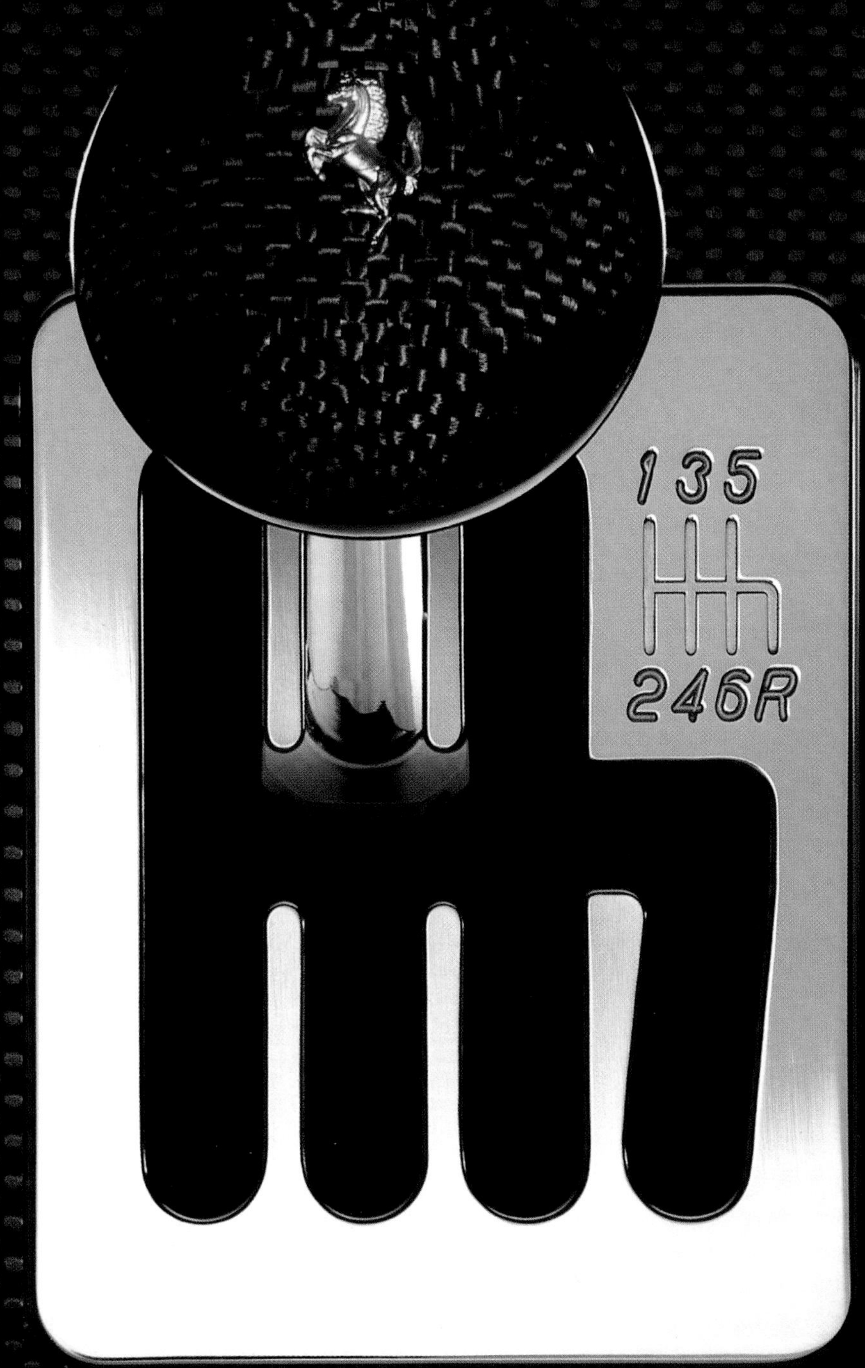
135
246R

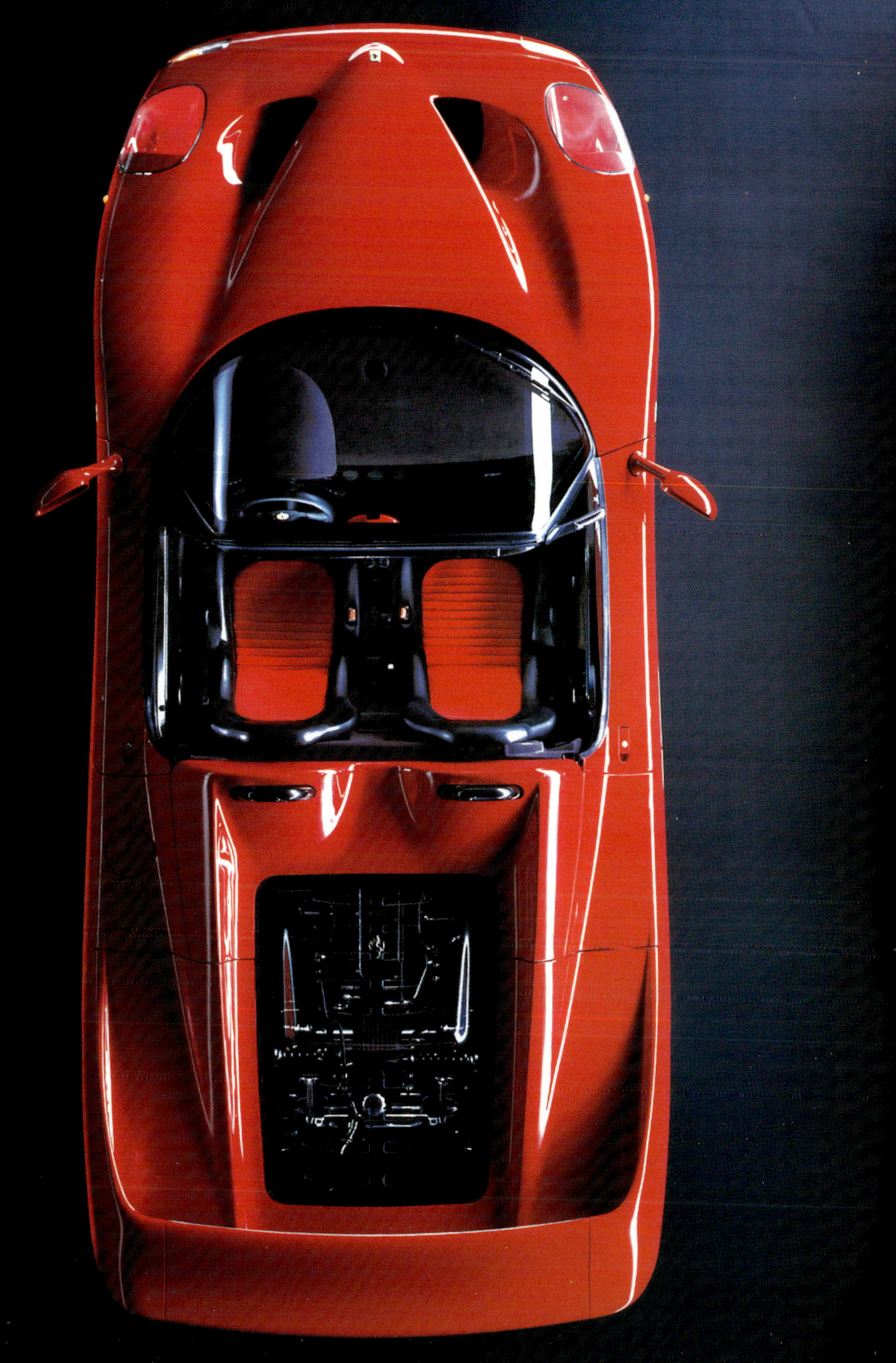

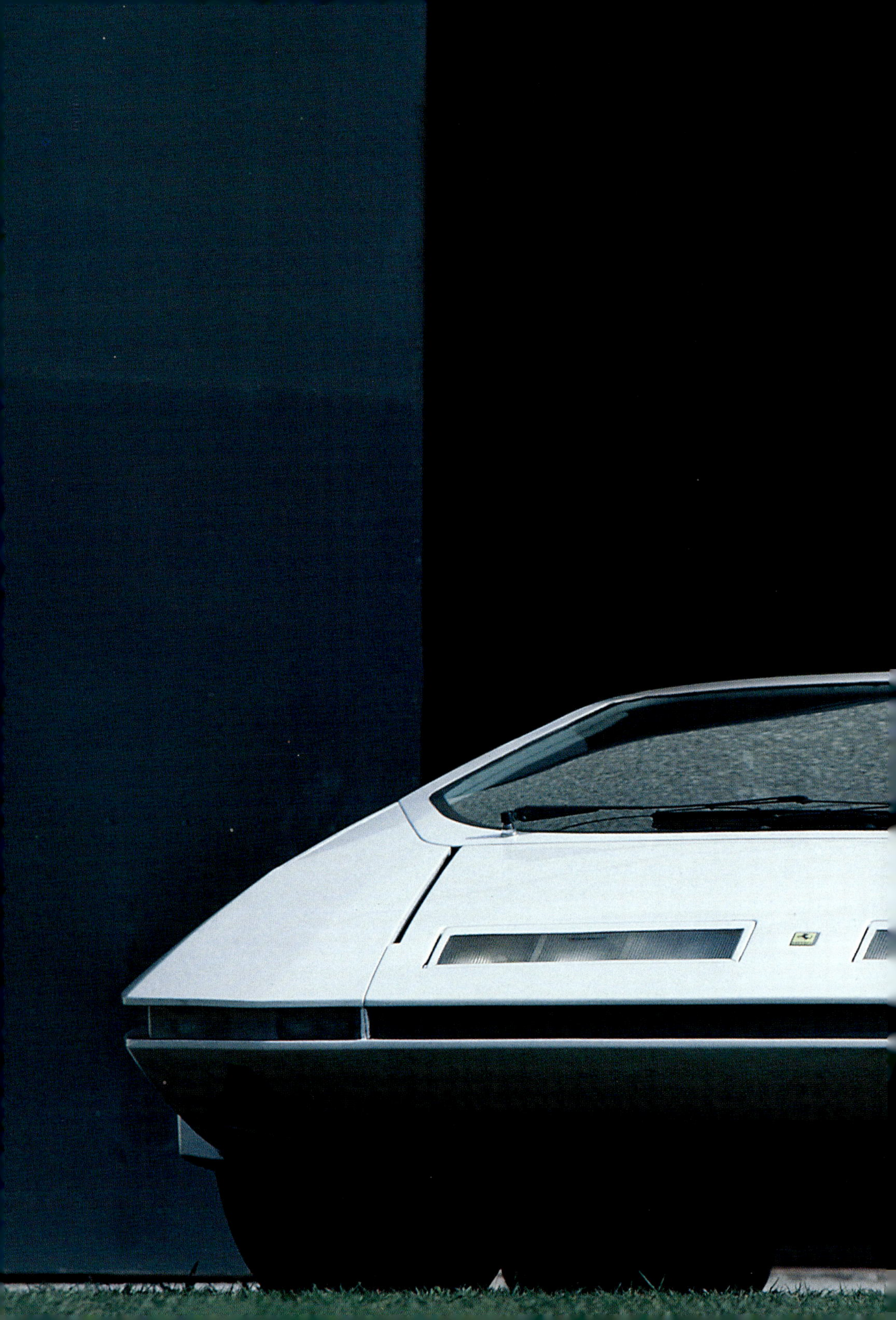

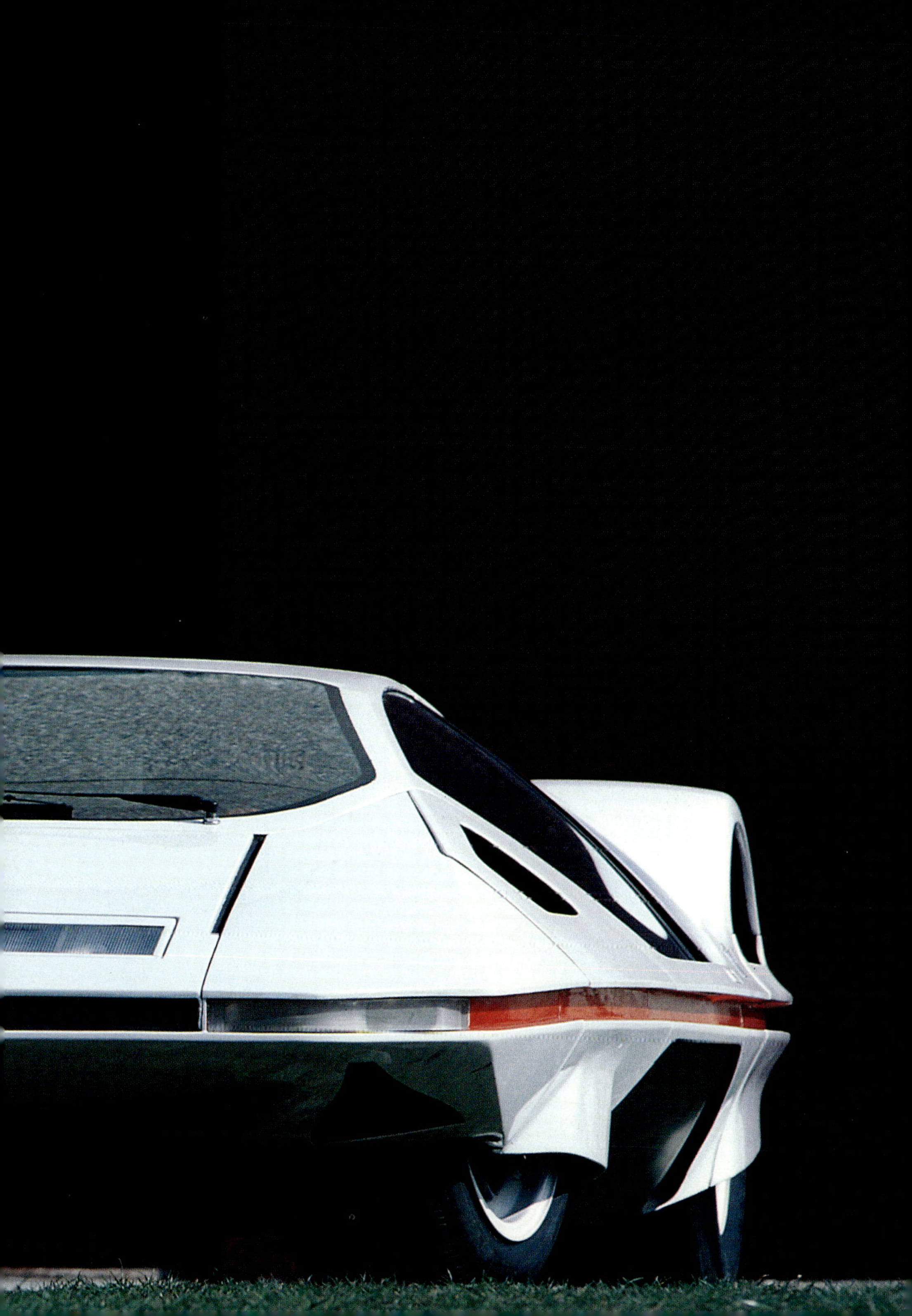

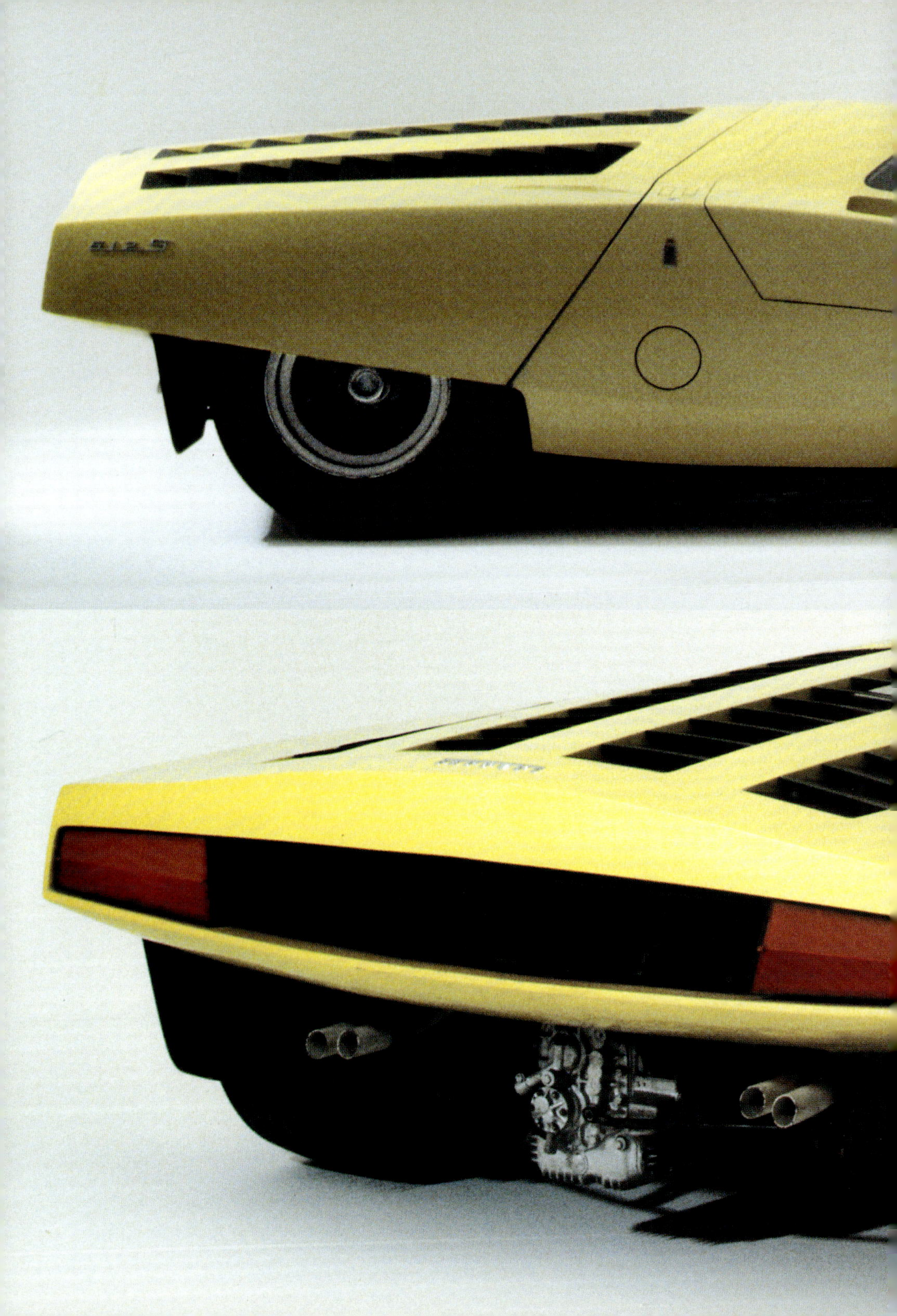

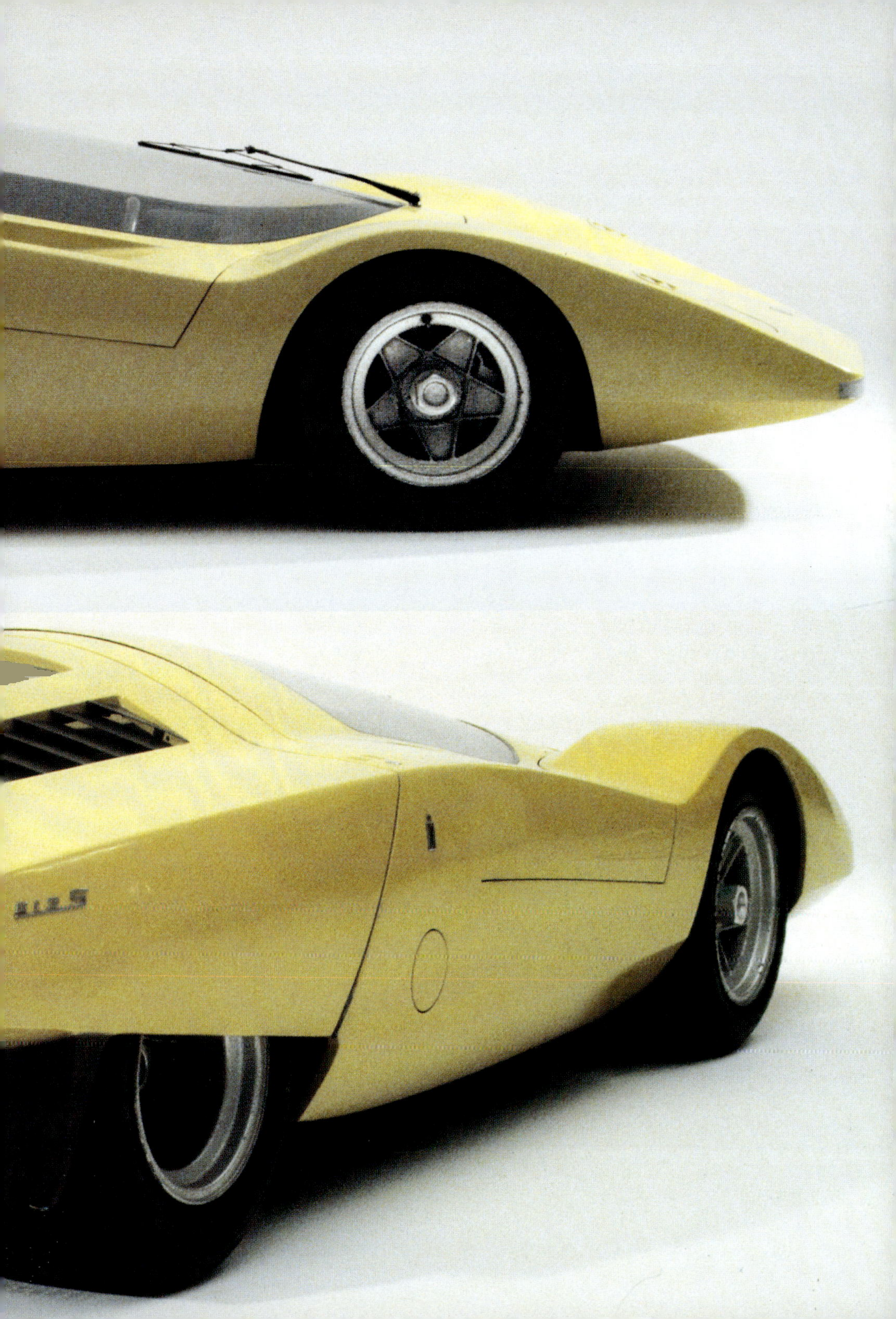

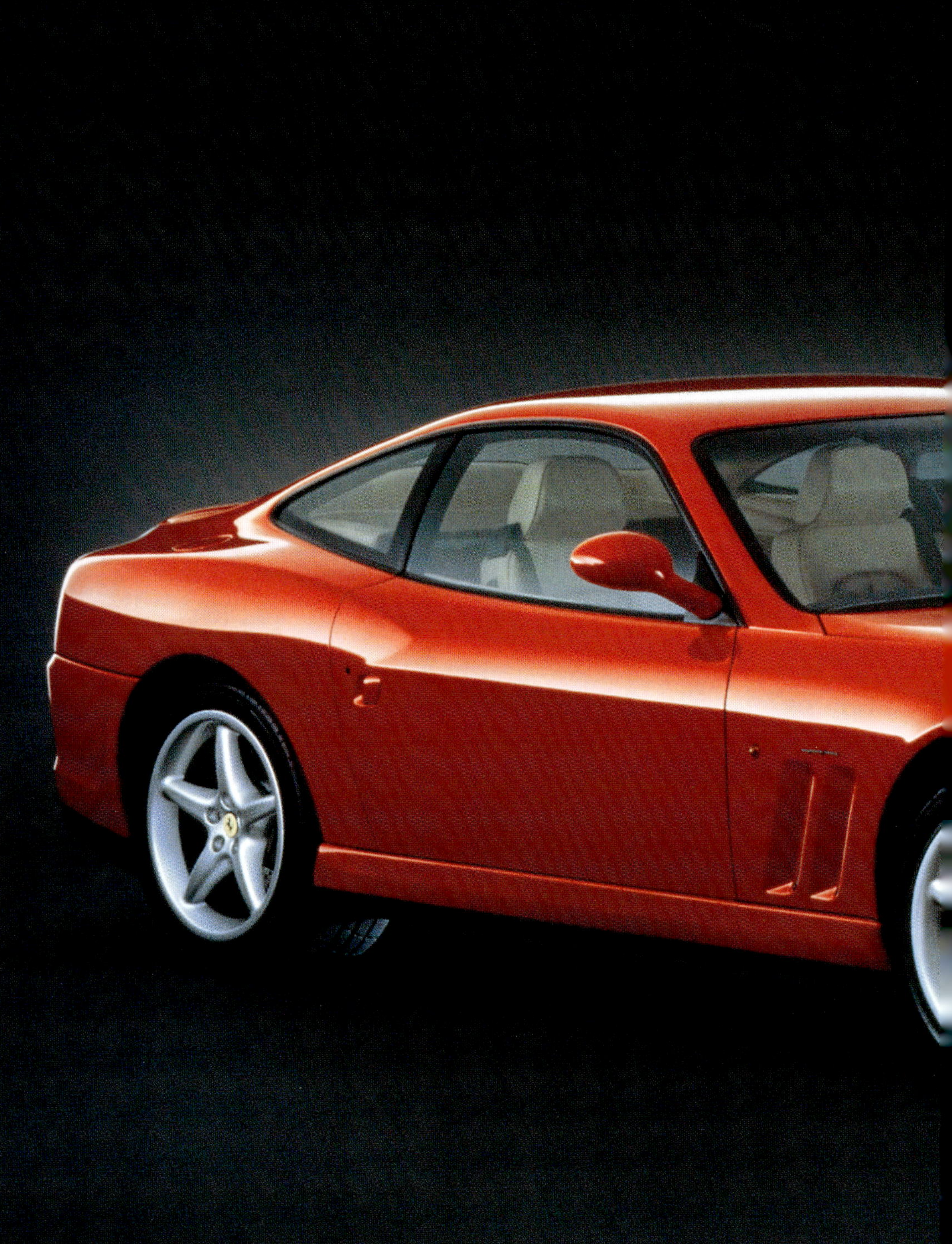

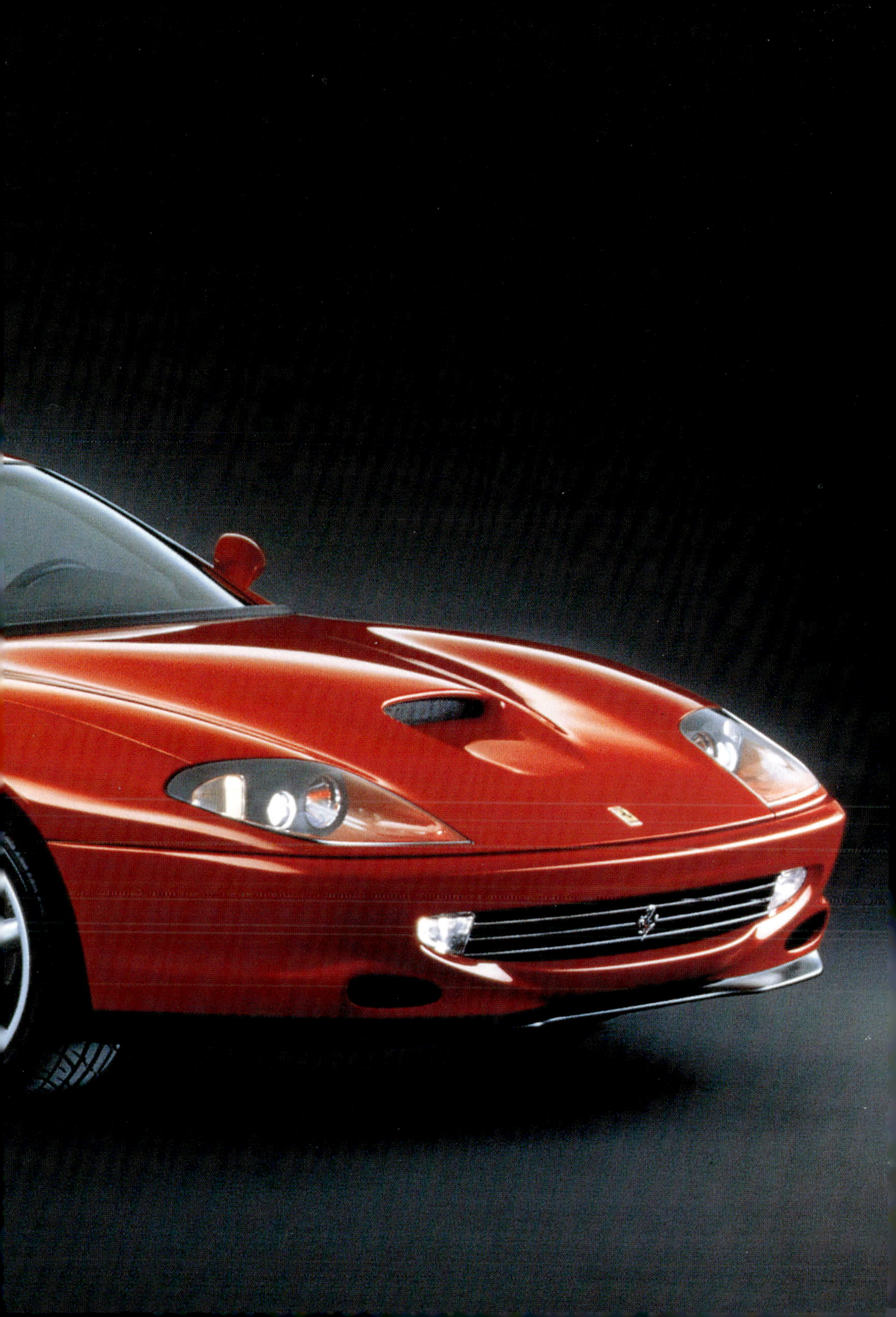

Ferrari & Pininfarina Models

1952: 212 Inter cabriolet (2 versions)

1953: 212 Inter coupe
250 Mille Miglia coupe
340 Mille Miglia coupe
342 America cabriolet (2 versions)
342 America coupe (2 versions)
212 Inter coupe (last version)
166 Mille Miglia Berlinetta
375 America coupe
375 Mille Miglia coupe (1st version)
375 Mille Miglia Spider (2 versions)
250 Europa coupe (2 versions)

1954: 500 Mondial Spider
375 Plus Spider
375 Mille Miglia coupe
(2nd to 4th versions)
250 Europa coupe
(3rd and 4th versions)
250 Europa cabriolet
375 Mille Miglia Spider (3rd version)
250 Monza Spider
750 Sport Spider
500 Mondial Berlinetta
250 GT coupe
375 Mille Miglia Berlinetta

1955: 375 Mille Miglia Berlinetta
(2nd version)
250 GT coupe (2nd to 6th versions)
375 Mille Miglia coupe (5th version)
375 America coupe (2nd version)
375 America Spider

1956: 250 GT coupe (7th and 8th versions)
410 Super America coupe (2 versions)
410 SA Super Fast I

1957: 250 GT Spider (3 versions)
250 GT cabriolet
250 GT coupe (9th version)
410 Super America coupe SF

1958: 250 GT coupe (10th to 16th versions)
410 Super America coupe (3rd version)

1959: 250 GT coupe (17th version)
250 Testarossa spider
410 Super America coupe (4th and 5th versions)
250 Berlinetta "interim"

1960: 250 GT cabriolet (2nd and 3rd versions)
400 Super America cabriolet (2 versions)
250 Berlinetta SWB 1
250 GT spider (3rd version)
400 SA Super Fast II
250 GT coupe 2+2 (3 versions)

1961: Berlinetta SWB 2
250 GT coupe 2+2 (4th version)
400 Super America coupe SF II
400 Super America coupe
400 Super America cabriolet
(3rd version)
250 GT Le Mans Berlinetta
250 GT coupe special (2 versions)

1962: 400 SA Super Fast III
250 GT cabriolet (4th version)
400 Super America cabriolet
(4th version)
400 SA Super Fast IV
400 Super America coupe
(2nd and 3rd versions)

1963: 250 GT Berlinetta (3 versions)
400 Super America coupe (4th and 5th versions)
250 GT coupe 2+2 (5th version)
330 Le Mans Berlinetta
250 Le Mans Berlinetta (2nd version)

1964: 330 GT coupe 2+2
500 Super Fast
275 GTS spider
275 GTB Berlinetta

1965: 330 GT coupe 2+2 (2nd version)
275 GTS spider (2nd version)
275 GTB Berlinetta (2nd version)

275 GTB Berlinetta special
275 GTB Berlinetta aerodynamic
250 Le Mans Berlinetta special
Dino Berlinetta special
275 Spider NART

1966: 275 GTB/4 Berlinetta
365 California cabriolet
330 GTC coupe
330 GTS Spider
365 P Berlinetta
Dino Berlinetta GT

1967: 365 P II Berlinetta
330 GTC coupe special
Dino Berlinetta
365 GT coupe 2+2
Dino 206 GT coupe

1968: Dino 206 GT coupe (2nd version)
250 P 5 Berlinetta
Dino 206 GT Berlinetta
365 GTB/4 Daytona
P 6 Berlinetta

1969: 365 GTS Spider
365 GTC coupe (2nd version)
365 GTS/4 Daytona Spider
365 GTB/4 coupe special
512 S Berlinetta special

1970: 512 S Modulo

1971: 365 GTC/4 coupe
365 GTB/4 Daytona
BB Berlinetta boxer (prot.)

1972: Dino 246 GTS Spider
365 GT/4 coupe 2+2

1973: 365 GT/4 BB Berlinetta

1974: CR 25

1975: 308 GTB Berlinetta

1976: BB 512 Berlinetta
400 automatic

1977: 308 GTB coupe special
308 GTS Spider

1980: Mondial 8 coupe 2+2
Pinin berlina

1981: BB 512 i Berlinetta

1982: 400 i coupe 2+2
208 turbo Berlinetta

1983: 208 turbo Spider
Mondial cabriolet 2+2

1984: GTO Berlinetta
Testarossa Berlinetta

1985: 412 coupe 2+2
328 GTB Berlinetta
328 GTS Spider
Mondial 3,2 coupe
Mondial 3,2 cabriolet

1986: Turbo GTB Berlinetta
Turbo GTS Spider
Testarossa Spider

1987: F 40
I cruscotti

1989: 348 Berlinetta
348 cabriolet
Mythos (Pininfarina *concept car*)

1992: 512 TR Berlinetta
456 GT Berlinetta

1993: 348 Spider

1994: F355 Berlinetta
F512M Berlinetta

1995: F50

1996: 550 Maranello Berlinetta

The various versions correspond to modifications to the body. The differences may be minor, such as a change to the air intake, or so substantial that the car is altered entirely. When the model number does not change, the engine characteristics remain identical.

Ferrari & Pininfarina

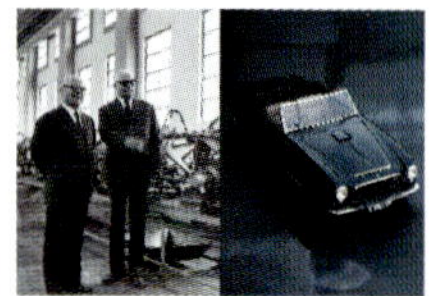

The first model. The Ferrari 212 Inter (1952) marked the beginning of the fruitful collaboration between Enzo Ferrari and Battista Pininfarina. This two-seater cabriolet sported an imposing radiator grille reminiscent of the single-seater Ferraris, world champions of the day. The 212 Inter has become one of the most coveted classics. Left: © Pininfarina Archives. Right: © Peter Vann.

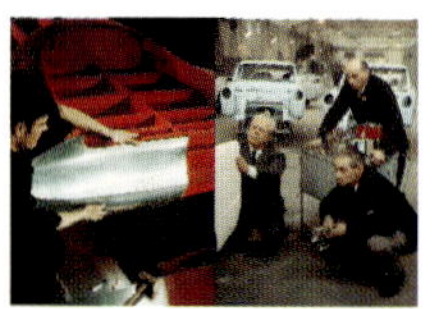

Custom-made quality in the automotive industry. Finishing touches were added by hand in the Pininfarina design studios. © Pininfarina Archives.
Until the last days of his life, Battista Pininfarina loved to linger in his workshops, mingling with his workers. He was not the type to dominate the conversation with his own ideas about style. © Pininfarina Archives.

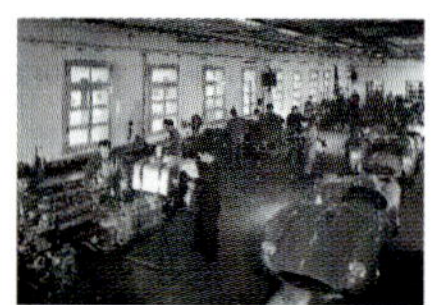

Haute couture workshops. The first car officially to bear the Ferrari name was the 125S in 1947. Most cars produced at that time by the Ferrari workshops in Maranello were immediately serviced for racing. © D.R.

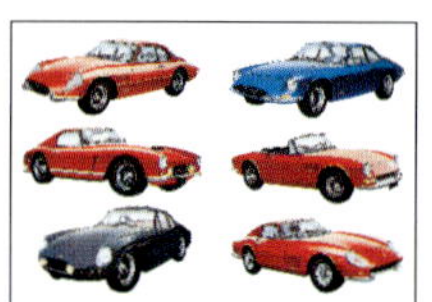

The nineteen-sixties. Left: 400 Superamerica from 1961 to 1964, V-12, 3967cc; 250 GT Berlinetta SWB 1959–1962, V-12, 2953cc; Le Mans Berlinetta Sperimentale, 1961, V-12, 2953cc. Right: 500 Superfast, 1964–1966, V-12, 4963cc; 275 GTS, 1964–1966, V-12, 3285cc; 275 GTB, 1964–1966, V-12, 3285cc. © D.R.

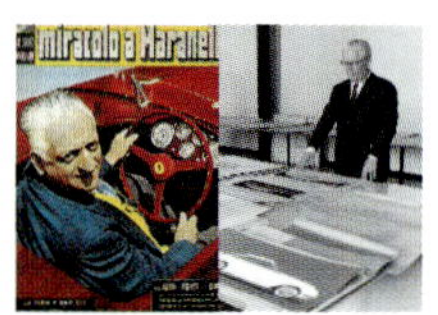

"Miracle in Maranello": This headline appeared in the Italian press in February, 1955 when Enzo Ferrari, *l'Ingeniere*, agreed to pose behind the wheel of one of his cars fitted with the already celebrated prancing horse emblem. © D.R.
Battista Pininfarina had been immersed in the automobile industry since his early childhood. He acquired his love for shapes and lines in the small auto workshop opened by his brothers. © Pininfarina Archives.

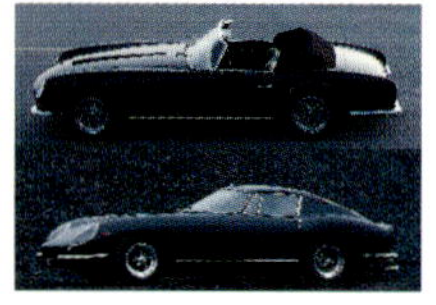

Flawless details. Cabriolet or coupe, the 275 GTB/4 masterpiece exhibited the genius of Pininfarina, whose signature embodied the finest of details. This model left its admirers speechless with the beauty of its slightly protruding rear fenders and the perfect design of the hood's "upper lip." © Peter Vann.

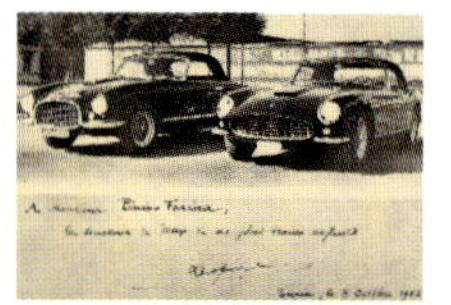

Second to none. In October 1955 King Leopold of Belgium, an admirer and car connoisseur, did not hesitate to praise the genius of Turin for creating such jewels as the Ferrari 340 America (1953) and the 250 GT (1954). © Pininfarina Archives.

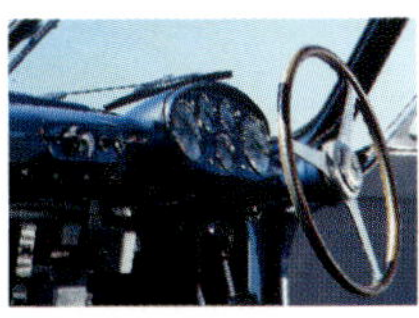

The finishing touches. When Enzo Ferrari and Battista Pininfarina finally decided to collaborate, their commitment was absolute. The designer from Turin had carte blanche to adorn the chassis and engines delivered from Ferrari. A Ferrari bodied by Pininfarina is instantly recognizable not only from its "P" badge, but also from such fine details as those found in the cockpit of this 375 Mille Miglia configured for racing. © Peter Vann.

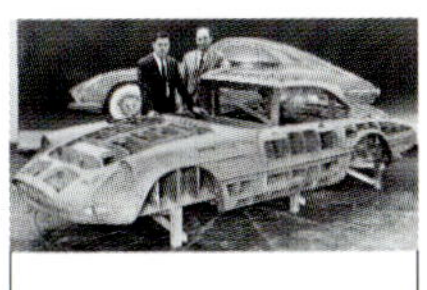

The new generation. Sergio Pininfarina and Renzo Carli took over the family business from Battista Pininfarina. They are photographed in front of a model for the Ferrari 250 GT. © Pininfarina Archives.

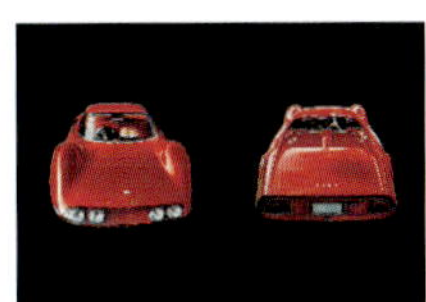

The balance between tribute and innovation. The Dino was one of the greatest projects undertaken by the Ferrari-Pininfarina partnership. Ferrari's goal was to complete as closely as possible the design begun by Dino Ferrari, the son of the famous *l'Ingeniere*. For Pininfarina, the objective was not only to design a body, but also to convince his partner to agree to an innovative mid-mounted engine. © Pininfarina Archives.

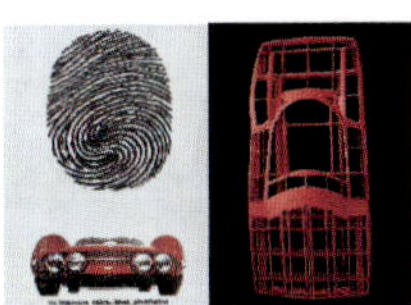

The imprint of a style. What best symbolizes the Pininfarina imprint left on most Ferrari models? Shown here, a special Dino Berlinetta presented at the 1965 Paris Auto Show. This car was a forerunner to the famous Dino 206 GT designed soon after by the Pininfarina sons. © Pininfarina Archives. All Ferraris begin as wood mock-ups. A full-scale working model is displayed vertically in the entrance to Pininfarina's Turin headquarters. © Bernard Asset.

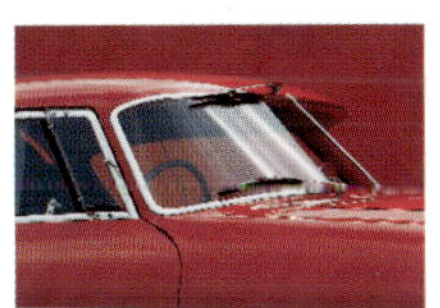

The power of invention. A racing car should come fitted with accessories worthy of its rank. Only the most talented stylists can turn a side deflector, the curve of the drip molding, or the sweep of the windshield into a thing of beauty. © Peter Vann.

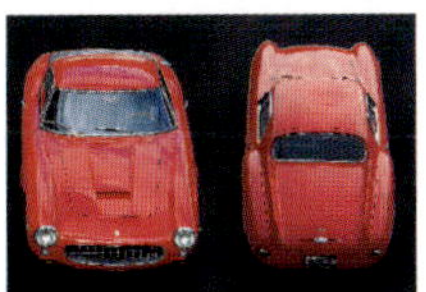

Between the race track and the road. Pininfarina paid special attention to the aerodynamics of the Ferrari 250 (1953), which was the forerunner of a multitude of models, ranging from the GT SWB (short wheel base) to the GT Special, a racing design with more aggressive lines than the touring version. Photos © Bernard Asset

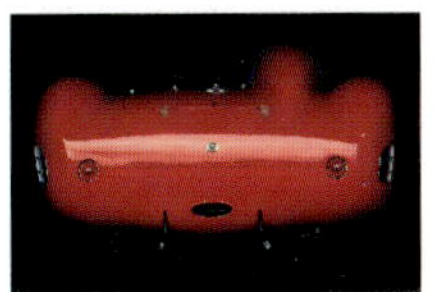

The red Testarossa. The Spider Ferrari 250 Testarossa remains among the most, if not the single most, famous Ferrari racing models. For the 1959 season, Pininfarina revised the design of this enormous beast to make it more standard and efficient. The 250 Testarossa was driven for the first time by the Frenchman Jean Behra at the Sebring 12-hour race. © Peter Vann.

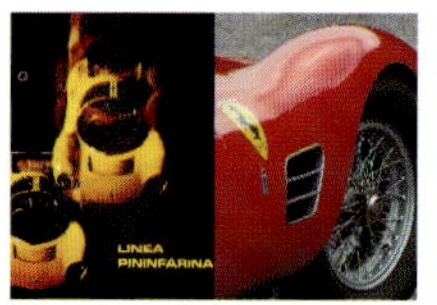

The Pininfarina signature, at the edge of the indefinable, placed any car shaped with its characteristic lines in a class of its own. At the end of the 1950s, the celebrated Testarossa, which got its name from its red-painted cylinder-head covers, would play a major role in enhancing Ferrari's racing reputation. Adding a few details to this racing monster, Pininfarina made his contribution to its racing and technological success. © Pininfarina Archives.

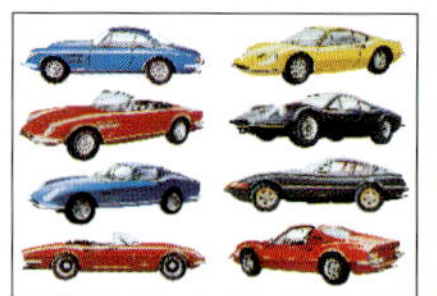

Racing elegance. Left: 330 GTC 1965–1967, V-12 3967cc; 330 GTS 1966, V-12, 3968cc; 275 GTB4 1966–1968, V-12, 3285cc; 365 California, 1966, V-12, 4390cc.
Right: Dino 206 GT 1967–1969, V-6, 1968cc; Dino 246 GT 1969-1974, V-6 2418cc; 365 GTB/4 1966-1968, V-12, 3285cc; Dino 246 GTS, 1972–1974, V-6, 2418cc. © D.R.

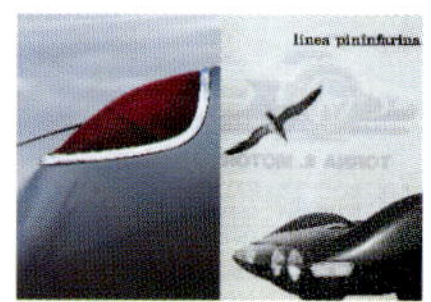

Attention to lines. This tail light on the upper curve of the fender was an innovation that was added to most 1957 Ferrari 250 GT models. © Peter Vann. The Pininfarina signature suggests that this Dino, with its strange nose, could travel any road as confidently as an Albatross flying freely in the sky. © Pininfarina Archives.

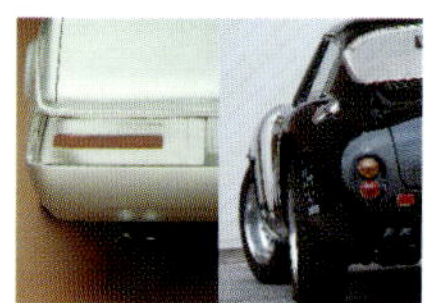

Development. Detailed view of the Pinin's tail light. This comfortable Berlinetta, created for the fiftieth anniversary of the Turin company, was supposed to be powered by a large V-12 Ferrari engine, but Enzo Ferrari vetoed the idea: since this design departed too far from his vision, the Pinin never went past the prototype phase. © Pininfarina Archives. This Ferrari 250 GT coupe, like many other Pininfarina creations, was graced with rounded lines. © Peter Vann.

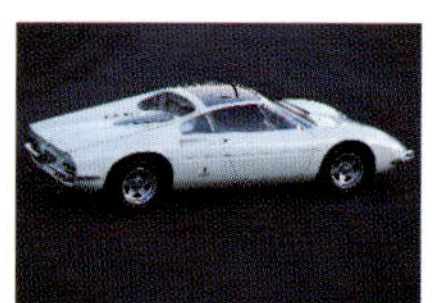

Bold design. The 365 P was presented by Pininfarina as one of the most sensational automobiles of all time. Its chassis—based on a 4390 cm^3 sports model—was in the center of the car, just behind the driver. The driver's seat was also in the center of the car, with passengers seated on either side. The 365P was inspired in part by the Dino prototype. © Pininfarina Archives.

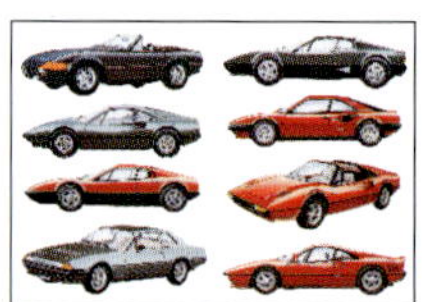

The nineteen-seventies. Left: 365 GTS/4, 1971, V-12, 4390cc; 308 GTB, 1975, 90° V-8, 2926cc; 365 BB (Boxer), 1973–1976, horizontally opposed 12 cyl., 4390cc; 400 GT Automatic 1976, V-12, 4823cc. Right: BB 512 (Berlinetta Boxer), 1976, horizontally opposed 12 cyl. 4942cc; Mondial 8, 1980, 90° V-8, 2926cc; 308 GTS, 1977, 90° V-8, 2926cc; GTO, 1984, 90° V-8, 2855cc; © D.R.

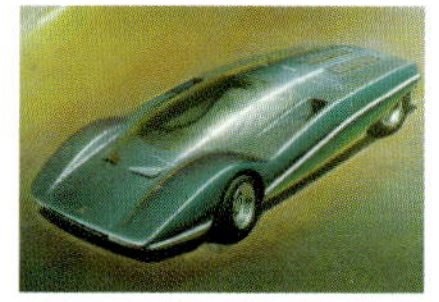

Advanced technology. Conforming with 1970s style, Pininfarina explored new lines with the Ferrari 512 S. This design was determined with the help of wind tunnel testing, undertaken in cooperation with the Polytechnic Institute of Turin. © Pininfarina Archives.

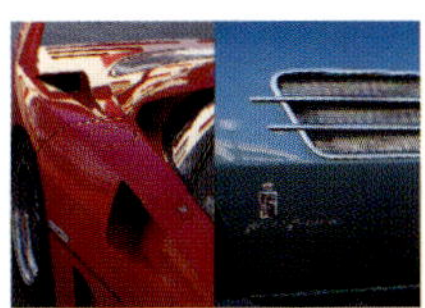

Designed for speed. Aerodynamic design to ensure the flow of air across the radiators, located on the side of the F40 model of the late 1980s. Identical, but less detailed work, for the front fender of a 1957 Ferrari 410 Superamerica. Photos © Peter Vann.

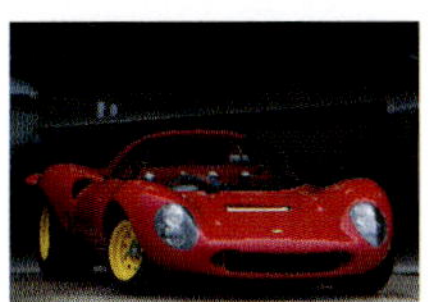

The curves. When car designers seek perfection the result can sometimes provoke people to caress the curves of these cold monsters just to calm their excitement. © Peter Vann.

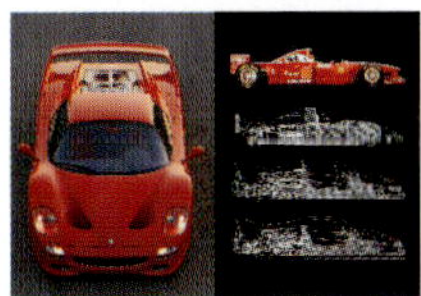

The metamorphosis of a car. The 1995 Ferrari F50 (left-hand page) was inspired directly by Ferrari's experience with Formula 1 cars. With this unusual Grand Touring car, the design studio of Pininfarina and Ferrari together took on the challenge of fusing touring car styling with the performance of a one-seater Grand Prix car. Left: © Peter Vann. Right: © Pininfarina Archives.

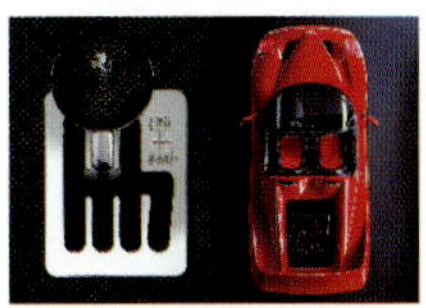

Tradition and advanced technology. The F50 was an enormous feat of advanced technology. The aerodynamic design of this car was produced after extensive wind tunnel testing, conducted in collaboration with Pininfarina. The chief designers were not willing to sacrifice comfort to improve the rigidity of the body. As a result, this car combined the ultimate in handling with the élan of a 4.7 liter V-12 engine with over 500 horsepower. © Ferrari Archives.

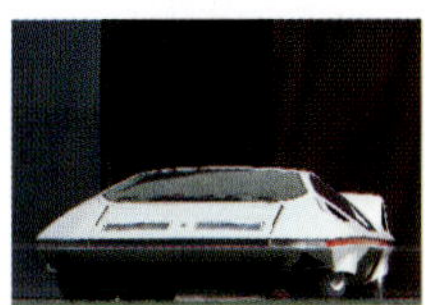

Concept car. A true laboratory of style, the Pininfarina offices served as design studios for the creative minds of the automotive world, where they were able to produce concept cars. The PF Modulo with its futuristic lines was designed for a racing chassis. While based on the principles of the 512 S, this model explored ultra-modern features. © Peter Vann.

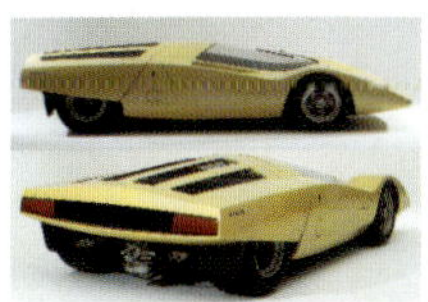

Futuristic models. Inspired by the CanAm series racing prototype, the Berlinetta 512S was only 98 centimeters in height. The side panels featured air vents to cool the radiators and the entire windshield slanted forward to allow entry into the two-seater cockpit. The rear-mounted transmission and gear box are barely concealed. © Pininfarina Archives.

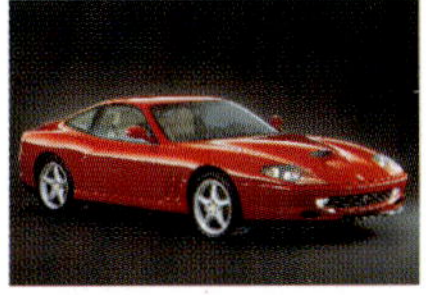

Looking toward the millennium. Presented at the 1996 Paris Auto Show, the F550 Maranello, the result of an intense collaborative effort between the two great houses, met with great success. This Berlinetta marks the return of a front-mounted engine, flaunting itself as the proud heir of the Testarossa. At the dawn of the twenty-first century, the Maranello offers the ultimate in performance and sheer delight to anyone who drives it. © Ferrari Archives.

The publishers would like to thank the House of Pininfarina, in particular: Lorenza Pininfarina and Lorenzo Ramaciotti as well as the House of Ferrari and in particular: Antonio Ghini and Antonella Leoni. We also wish to thank Patrick Lifshitz, Hervé Fontaine, Antoine Prunet, Peter Vann, Béatrice Dhenin and Bernard Asset who contributed to this work